DO-IT-YOURSELF ENCYCLOPEDIA

*A Practical Guide
to Home Improvement,
Repairs and Decorating
containing special material from
The Family Handyman
Do-It-Yourself Encyclopedia
and Family Circle.*

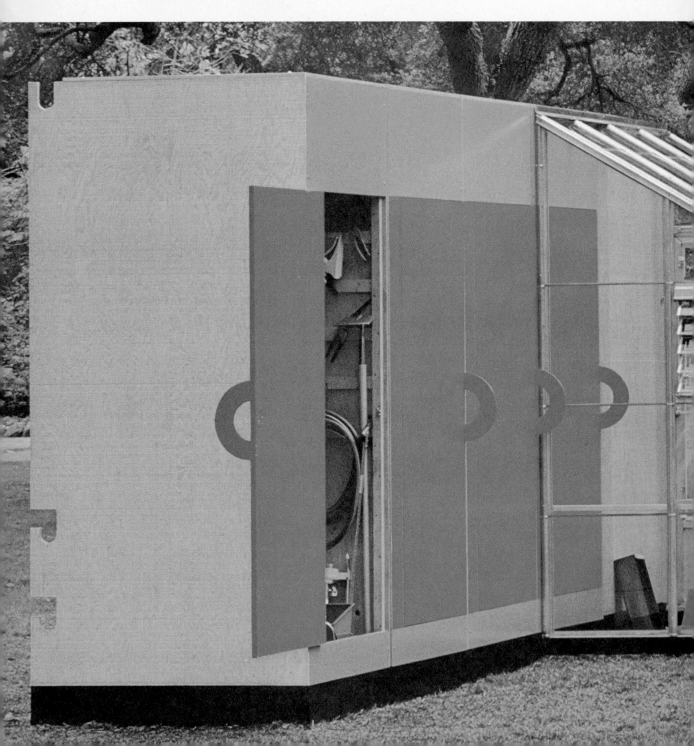

Family Circle®

DO-IT-YOURSELF

ENCYCLOPEDIA

VOLUME **12** Out-Pat

ROCKVILLE HOUSE PUBLISHERS, INC.

GARDEN CITY, NEW YORK 11530

Acknowledgments

The editors of this series would like to express their thanks and appreciation to the following for their assistance in preparing special sections within this encyclopedia, for their technical advice, and for photographs, art, charts and plans.

Alsynite Co. of America • American Plywood Assn. • Baker Brush Co. • Robert C. Cleveland-Alpha • Harold Davis • George de Gennaro • Douglas Fir Plywood Assn. • E Z Paintr Corp. • Alan Hicks • Taylor Lewis & Associates • Lightolier, Inc. • Vincent Lisanti • Manor Crafts • Martin Fabrics Corp. • Masonite Corp. • Monsanto Chemical Co. • National Plant, Varnish & Lacquer Assn. • George Nordhausen • Ozite Carpet Co. • PPG Industries • Plasti-Kote • Portland Cement Assn. • Red Devil Tools • O. Philip Roedel • Steber Mfg. Co. • Structural Clay Products Institute • Valspar Corp. • Valspar Paints • Hans Van Nes • Lester Waiker • Wilson Imperial Co.

Published by arrangement with
The Family Circle, Inc.,
a subsidiary of The New York Times Media Company, Inc.

Outdoor Furniture

There are many attractive pieces of furniture which the handyman can build for outdoor living. During the winter months, you can tinker in the workshop and when spring comes, you can have comfortable and useful outdoor furniture.

When making furniture—tables and chairs—for outdoor use, you must select the wood carefully and then finish it to prevent warping or rotting outdoors. Redwood and cedar are particularly good for outdoor use since they are decay-resistant. You can, however, use any of the other woods, including exterior plywood and tempered hardboard, if you apply a protective finish coat.

For construction techniques and details to help you make some of the pieces shown here, see the section on *FURNITURE*.

Aluminum and Redwood Table and Benches

Here's a welcome addition to any outdoor living center—a dining table made of weather- and decay-resistant redwood combined with aluminum. Once you have mastered the technique of working with Do-It-Yourself Aluminum, you will find it comparatively easy to make this unusual combination.

The table should be built so that the top is 30" from the floor. Four sets of legs are made of angle aluminum and joined to the redwood slat table. The top is made of 2x4's and the legs are braced to the top with aluminum rod, bolted to the legs and screwed to the underside of the table. A convenient size for this table is about 34"x72".

The benches, also made of redwood 2x4's and aluminum, have legs similar to the table. Each bench

1589

The concept of outdoor "rooms" is accentuated by the use of carpeting and furniture which is as much at home here as it would be indoors. Double your money's worth by purchasing furniture which is weatherproof for outdoor use, yet handsome enough to be at home indoors also.

*Photos courtesy
Ozite Carpet Company*

1590

Finished table and benches—same leg design is used for both benches and table.

should be about 15″ high, 72″ long and about 12″ wide. Construction of the benches is similar to that of the table, except that the aluminum rod is fastened diagonally from the center of the legs toward the center of the benches.

Take-Apart Table and Benches

Four 4′x8′ panels of ¾″ exterior grade plywood are the basic lumber requirements for making this practical outdoor dining table and benches plus a convenient cabinet to hold charcoal, cooking equipment and the rest of the barbecue gear. When the summer's over, you can take the table apart and store it in the garage or basement. In this way, it takes practically no room at all.

To make the table, benches and cabinet, cut the four panels of fir plywood as shown in the accom-panying sketches. Cut each piece to the size specified and sand all edges smooth. Assemble the various units, countersinking all screw heads and nails.

The exposed grain edges of all the plywood pieces should be filled with wood filler and then all surfaces should be given a protective finish.

Also see section on *FURNITURE FINISHING*.

You can make this take-apart plywood table, benches and cabinet over a single week-end and then enjoy their use all summer long, summer after summer.

Finished view of the handy cabinet.

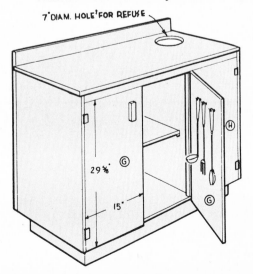

Materials Needed	
TABLE	
1 panel—¾″ exterior grade plywood	4′x8′
8′ lumber	1x1
4 hooks and eyes	
CABINET	
2 panels—¾″ exterior grade plywood	4′x8′
10′ lumber	2x4
4′ lumber	1x2
22′ lumber (or plywood scraps)	1x1
6 2″ narrow cabinet butt hinges	
3 bullet catches	
BENCH	
1 panel—¾″ exterior grade plywood	4′x8′
22′ lumber	1x1

7″ DIAM. HOLE FOR REFUSE

29⅝″

15″

1591

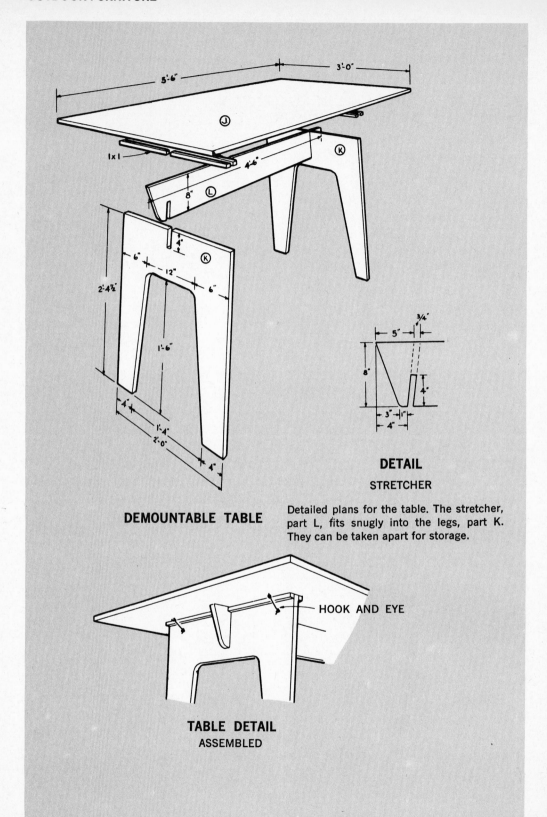

DEMOUNTABLE TABLE

DETAIL

STRETCHER

Detailed plans for the table. The stretcher, part L, fits snugly into the legs, part K. They can be taken apart for storage.

1592

HOOK AND EYE

TABLE DETAIL
ASSEMBLED

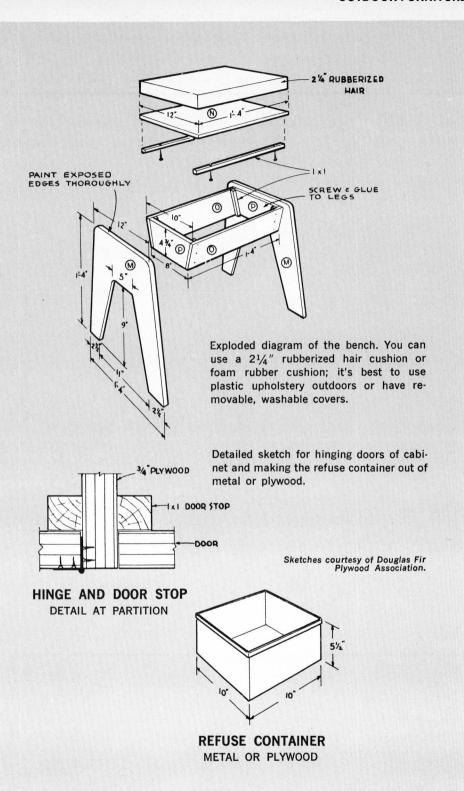

2¼" RUBBERIZED HAIR

12" Ⓝ 1'- 4"

1 x 1

SCREW & GLUE TO LEGS

PAINT EXPOSED EDGES THOROUGHLY

12"

10" Ⓞ Ⓟ

4¾" Ⓟ Ⓞ 1'-4"

8"

1'-4" Ⓜ Ⓜ

5"

9"

2½"

11"

1'-4"

2½"

Exploded diagram of the bench. You can use a 2¼" rubberized hair cushion or foam rubber cushion; it's best to use plastic upholstery outdoors or have re-movable, washable covers.

Detailed sketch for hinging doors of cabi-net and making the refuse container out of metal or plywood.

¾" PLYWOOD

1 x 1 DOOR STOP

DOOR

Sketches courtesy of Douglas Fir Plywood Association.

HINGE AND DOOR STOP
DETAIL AT PARTITION

5½"

10" 10"

REFUSE CONTAINER
METAL OR PLYWOOD

1593

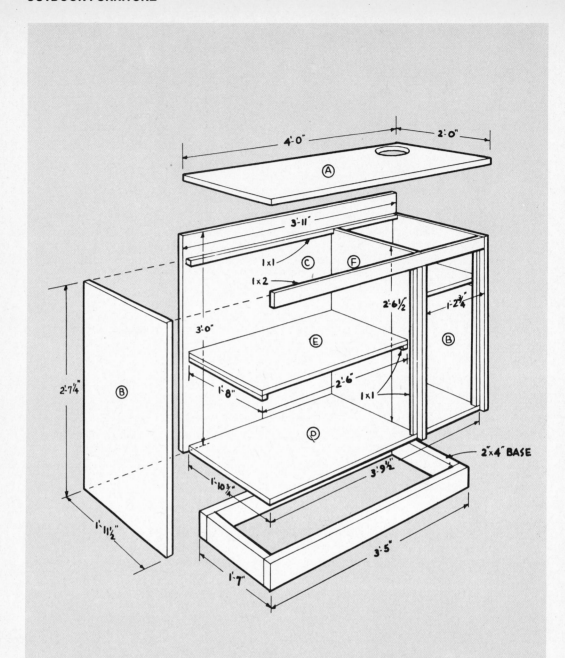

1594

Detailed view of cabinet construction.

Picnic Table and Benches

You can have fun all summer long —right in your own back yard—with a "no-tip" picnic table and benches. This 3′x6′ table is rugged and sturdy, made with a tempered hardboard top.

Plans include details for four benches so you and your family and guests can sit all around the table. When the set is not in use, the table and benches are easily stored as the smaller benches can be set over the longer benches and under the table.

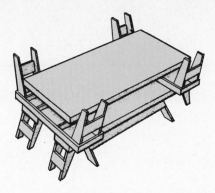

See how compactly you can store the table and benches when not in use.

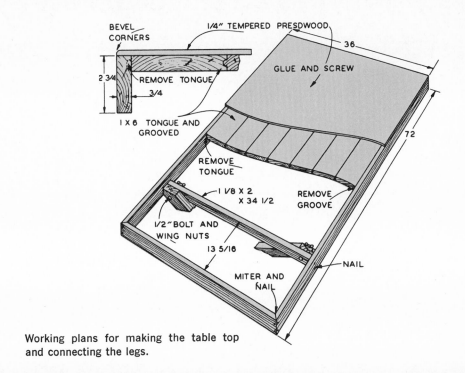

Picnic table with four benches features a tempered hardboard top.

BEVEL CORNERS

1/4" TEMPERED PRESDWOOD

36

GLUE AND SCREW

2 3/4

REMOVE TONGUE

3/4

1 X 6 TONGUE AND GROOVED

72

REMOVE TONGUE

REMOVE GROOVE

1 1/8 X 2 X 34 1/2

1/2" BOLT AND WING NUTS

13 5/16

NAIL

MITER AND NAIL

1595

Working plans for making the table top and connecting the legs.

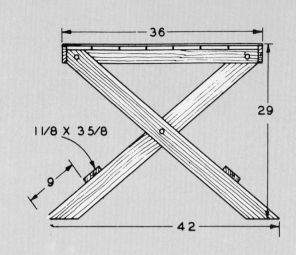

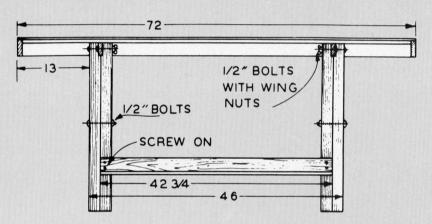

Front and side views showing basic dimensions of the table.

Front and end views of the benches. Note that two benches are made 72" long and two others are 48" long.

1596

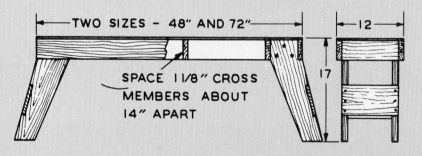

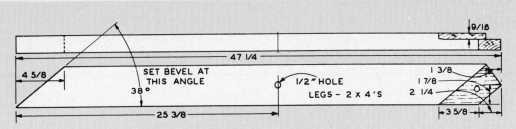

Detailed plans for table legs; make four.

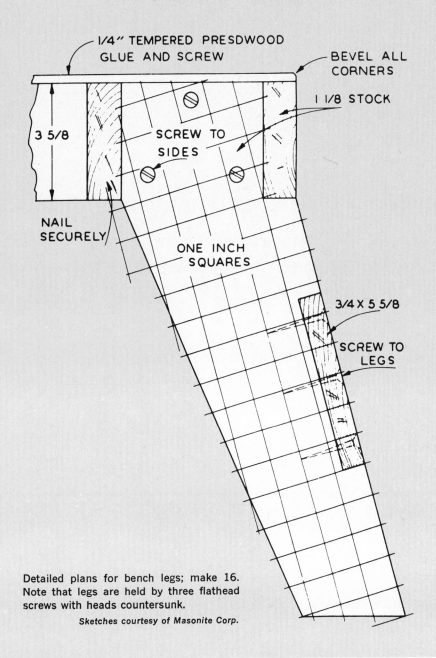

Detailed plans for bench legs; make 16.
Note that legs are held by three flathead
screws with heads countersunk.

Sketches courtesy of Masonite Corp.

1597

Make the top first. Use 1x6 tongue-and-groove lumber, which usually has a surface width of 5″ to 5¼″. This will vary, but the over-all width of the joined stock should be 34½″. Plane or saw off the tongue of one end board and the groove of the other end board. A power saw will do this very quickly.

Screw the 1x6 tongue and groove section to the 1⅓″x2″ cross ties, using flat head wood screws. These should be countersunk below the surface. It is best to drill the ½″ bolt hole in the cross ties before assembly. This is easier than drilling after pieces are assembled. Miter the corners of the ¾″ outer edge frame and nail on both ways.

Next; make the simple frame legs of 2x4's. The end of each leg is notched out ⁹⁄₁₆″ to receive the 1⅛″ top cross tie. One leg fits on one side of the tie and the other on the other side. It is best to make each leg assembly and then clamp to the top. Then make the lower leg cross braces, or ties. In this way, if there has been any variance in the dimensions of the lumber, you will automatically make the braces to fit. Then screw the braces into place.

Before applying the tempered hardboard (to table top, to bench, or to lawn chair), scrub cold water into the screen side with a stiff broom until it turns a dark chocolate brown color. Cover with a damp newspaper or tarpaulin and allow to remain for at least 24 hours.

After cutting the tempered hardboard to fit, apply a waterproof ad-

1598

Materials Needed				
PICNIC TABLE AND FOUR BENCHES STOCK: ¼″ TEMPERED HARDBOARD; PINE OR FIR LUMBER (All dimensions are for finished sizes)				
TABLE				
Name of part	No. Req.	Thickness	Width	Length
Legs	4	1⅝	3⅝	47¼
Leg tie	1	1⅛	3⅝	42¾
Leg tie	1	1⅛	3⅝	46
Top (flooring)	7	¾	6	70½
Top ties	2	1⅛	2	34½
Top side bands	2	¾	2¾	72
Top end bands	2	¾	2¾	36
Tempered hardboard top	1	¼	36	72
BENCHES—Two Short and Two Long				
Name of part	No. Req.	Thickness	Width	Length
Legs	16	1⅛	5⅝	18⅝
Cross ties and end bands	24	1⅛	3⅝	9¾
Side bands (long)	4	1⅛	3⅝	72
Sand bands (short)	4	1⅛	3⅝	48
Leg braces	8	¾	5⅝	9¾
Tempered hardboard seats	2	¼	12	72
Tempered hardboard seats	2	¼	12	48
HARDWARE				
Two, ½″ bolts 4″ long with nuts. Four, ½″ bolts 3″ long with wing nuts. Nails, 2″ wood screws. ¾″ long flat head brass wood screws to fasten hardboard.				

A sturdy garden bench, designed for simplified construction.

hesive to the screen side, place in position and screw to the wood top with ¾" flat head brass wood screws. Countersink the screw heads flush with or slightly below the surface. Screws should be placed 4" apart around the edges and 16" apart throughout the body of the panel.

To finish the table, apply a first coat of exterior grade primer or sealer. Then follow with two coats of exterior grade enamel. It will be easier if you disassemble table before finishing.

The Benches

Make the legs first. Be as careful as you can with the accuracy of your dimensions because the bench must be strong and sturdy, if it is to hold the number of people for which it is designed.

Then nail or screw together the outside frame of the 1⅛"x5⅝" stock. Screw one leg in each corner and then fit in the first cross brace, being sure that it fits snugly against the leg.

Nail this first cross brace in very securely. Then fasten the other cross braces. It is well to have them not less than 14" apart. The cross braces on the legs can then be screwed in.

Fit seats of ¼" tempered hardboard in place (see conditioning instructions noted previously) and screw them on in the same manner as for the table top, using flat head brass wood screws. Space screws 3" apart around the edges and 4" apart at cross braces.

Finish the same as for table.

Garden Bench

This sturdy garden bench is designed for simplified construction. It can be built by the do-it-yourselfer in about 1½ hours at a cost of under $15, using WWP-grade-trademarked fir.

Materials needed include one

1599

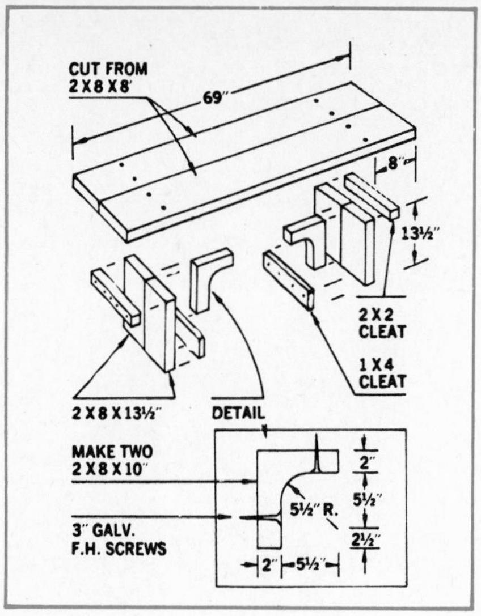
CUT FROM
2X8X8'
69"
8"
13½"
2X2
CLEAT
1X4
CLEAT
2X8X13½"
DETAIL
MAKE TWO
2X8X10"
3" GALV.
F.H. SCREWS
2"
5½" R.
5½"
2½"
2"
5½"

2x8x10′; one 2x8x8′; one 2x2x3′; one 1x4x3′; four 3″ galvanized flat head nails; and 12d galvanized nails.

The 2x8s are cut into two 69″ seat pieces and four 13½″ legs, along with two 10″ braces (see detail in drawing). Two 15″ cleats are cut from the 2x2; two more of the same size from the 1x4. Assembly of the bench is shown in the drawing. The unit is finished with a coating of water-repellent stain, applied according to manufacturer's directions.

Lawn Chair

The first step is to build the back, carefully following the diagram. Fasten the 3⁄16″ hardboard with washers and ¾″ oval head brass screws. Next cut out all the other parts. Assemble, using 1¼″ wood screws.

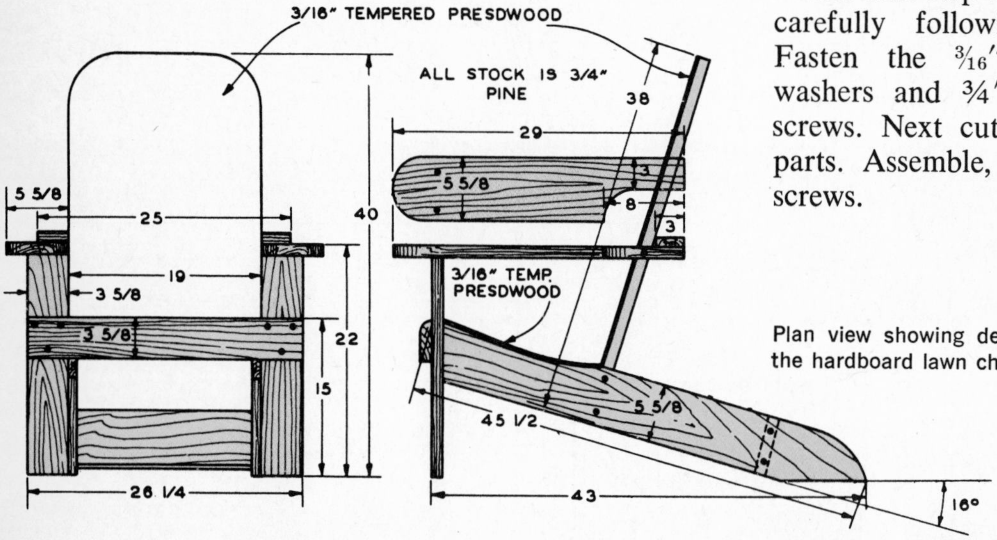
3/16" TEMPERED PRESDWOOD
ALL STOCK IS 3/4"
PINE
38
29
3
5 5/8
8
3
40
5 5/8
25
19
3 5/8
3 5/8
22
15
26 1/4
3/16" TEMP.
PRESDWOOD
45 1/2
5 5/8
43
16°

Plan view showing detailed dimensions of the hardboard lawn chair.

Part	Thickness	Width	Length
2 Legs	¾	3⅝	21¼
2 Side legs	¾	5⅝	45½
2 Arms	¾	5⅝	29
1 Front tie	¾	3⅝	26½
3 Seat cleats and cross brace	¾	2⅝	17½
1 Back leg brace	¾	5⅝	17½
1 Arm tie	¾	3	25
4 Anchor blocks	¾	3	4
1 Back, top	¾	5⅝	13¾
2 Back cross pieces	¾	3⅝	13¾
2 Back sides	¾	3⅝	38
1 Hardboard seat	3⁄16	19	17¼
1 Hardboard back	3⁄16	19	38

Metal crimp fasteners; 1¼″ No. 14 wood screws; ¾″ oval head brass wood screws with finishing washers to fasten hardboard.

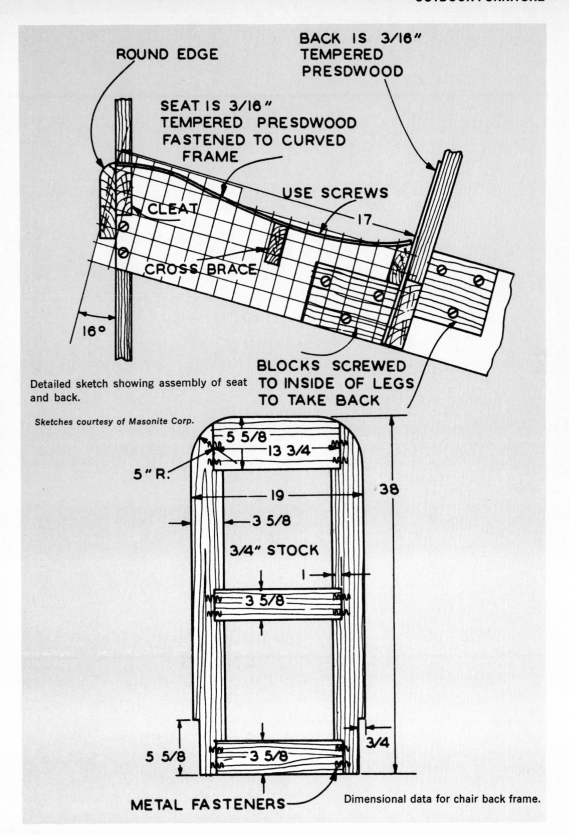

ROUND EDGE

BACK IS 3/16" TEMPERED PRESDWOOD

SEAT IS 3/16" TEMPERED PRESDWOOD FASTENED TO CURVED FRAME

USE SCREWS

CLEAT

17

CROSS BRACE

16°

BLOCKS SCREWED TO INSIDE OF LEGS TO TAKE BACK

Detailed sketch showing assembly of seat and back.

Sketches courtesy of Masonite Corp.

5 5/8

13 3/4

5" R.

19

38

3 5/8

3/4" STOCK

1

3 5/8

5 5/8

3 5/8

3/4

METAL FASTENERS

Dimensional data for chair back frame.

1601

The last step is fastening the hardboard seat. Do this by first joining the front edge to the recessed cleat so that it is even with the front cross piece. Sand or plane any minor irregularities. Then fasten the panel to the framework, starting from front and working toward the back as you bend the panel into place. Be sure to condition the hardboard before fastening. (See *"PICNIC TABLE* and *BENCHES."*)

Finishing: Follow recommendations for picnic table and benches described previously in this section.

Note: For best results, bevel or sand all exposed edges of hardboard after installation.

Plastic Webbing Chair

This attractive chair, woven in plastic webbing, can be used indoors as well as outdoors. It is a project for the more advanced handyman.

This webbing comes in many different colors and is very durable.

1602

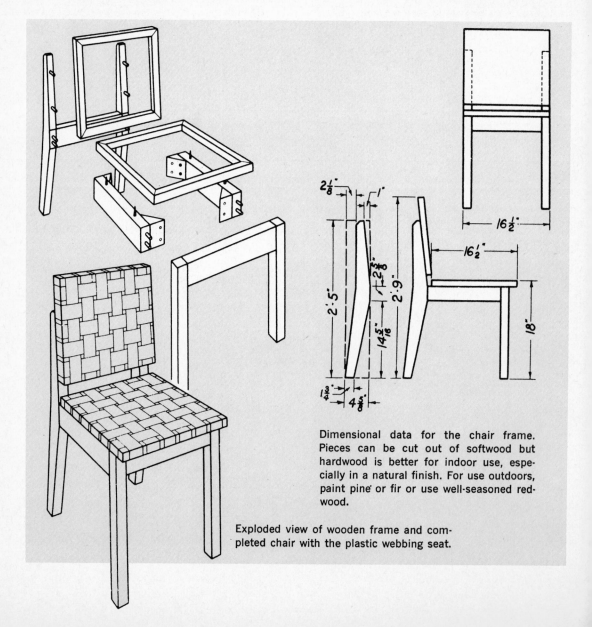

Dimensional data for the chair frame. Pieces can be cut out of softwood but hardwood is better for indoor use, especially in a natural finish. For use outdoors, paint pine or fir or use well-seasoned redwood.

Exploded view of wooden frame and completed chair with the plastic webbing seat.

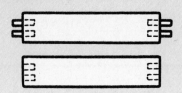

Front and rear braces are fastened to the legs with dowels.

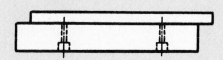

The frame for the plastic webbing seat is secured to the wooden frame by two countersunk flathead screws on each side.

After the frame has been assembled, it is best to clamp the entire assembly until the glue has dried.

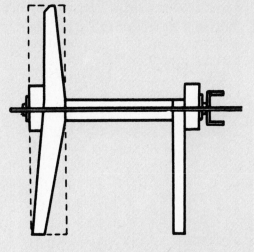

Sketches courtesy of Martin Fabrics Corp.

It is strong and sturdy and won't stretch; furthermore, it is moisture-proof and fade-resistant so that it can stay outdoors in any type of weather. The webbing itself is open weave to permit air to circulate through it and when laced on the chair, the seat is comfortable and airy. Plastic webbing is available in many hardware, variety and specialty stores and can be purchased by the yard in any color you desire.

1. *Layout*

a. Make a full size drawing of the front and side views on detail or brown wrapping paper.

b. Detail the joints in the open spaces on the drawing.

c. Mark out the locations for the webbing. If you have changed the dimensions of the chair for any rea-son, allow about ½″ between each strip.

2. *Cabinet work*

a. Mark saw cutting lines on rough stock.

b. Cut to lines leaving just enough for squaring and finishing operations. (Save the cut piece from the back legs to use them for cushions.) Check the sizes and angles by laying the cut pieces on your full size drawing.

c. Drill for dowels on side rails and legs. Use doweling jig or points to locate mating dowel locations. (See *BLIND DOWELING*.)

d. Glue the dowels into the rails.

e. Glue joints: Spread glue on surfaces and in the dowel holes to be joined.

Do the sides first; place cushion block and apply clamp. Stand the

1603

two sides next to each other and check for match. If necessary tap the front leg up or down so that the angles of the backs are the same. Then take up on the clamps and wipe off the excess glue.

Insert dowels in front and back rails and assemble chair on a flat surface. This will insure a chair which does not wobble.

f. Seat and back frames: The joints may be made—(1) mitered and blocked (2) mitered and splined (3) rabbeted or lapped.

g. Attaching seat to chair frame: Measure the diameter of the heads

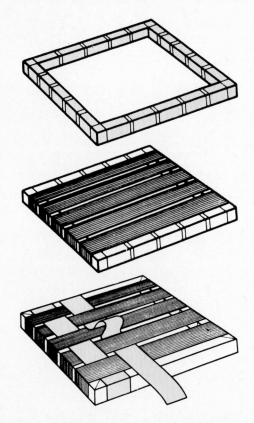

1604

Sketches courtesy of Martin Fabrics Corp.

To apply webbing—mark off the location of each of the strips on the frame. Attach the strips in one direction as specified in the working details. Then lace additional webbing at right angles to complete the chair seat.

of the screws to be used. Drill holes slightly larger and about ½″ deep on the under side of the side rails.

Drill holes the diameter of the shank of the screws to be used the rest of the way through the rails.

After webbing has been applied the seat can readily be attached to the frame.

h. Attaching the back to the frame: Locate the dowel holes so that they will come between strips of the webbing. Set dowels in uprights and then set back over them.

i. Rounding edges—All edges over which plastic webbing will pass should be sanded round. This will prolong the life of the webbing.

j. Finishing—All sanding, staining, shellacking or varnishing should be done at this time.

3. *Now you are ready to apply plastic webbing*

a. Mark out all locations for webbing on the insides of the seat and back frames.

b. Fold the ends back on all the strips which will be used on one side of the frame. Tack them in place. Stand the frame on its side to do this.

c. Lay the frame down on a workbench and let it hang out over the edge, clamp it down.

d. Stretch a strip of the attached webbing towards you and fold it down over the rail. Clamp it tight and tack it home on the under side. Continue this for all the other strips.

e. Do the same for the strips to be woven. This time simply weave them in whatever pattern you have selected.

Note: Stretching is not necessary but it does make a neater and firmer seat.

An example of economical landscape lighting.

4. *Final assembly*

Screw the seat and back in place. Put silent domes on the bottom of each leg to prevent splintering of the wood when the chair is moved.

Outdoor Lighting

There's a trace of bat or owl in all of us. Just enough so we like to be outdoors after dark, but not enough so we can get along without any light at all. You can give full play to the owl in you by wiring your outdoor living area for light. In many ways, outdoor wiring is easier than indoor wiring for most of the complications of indoor house wiring are absent.

You can light your patio and outdoor living area as well as any part of your property for some or all of many purposes. You can pinpoint a few spotlights for a night view of your garden from inside your home. You can illuminate your outdoor play-and-dining area. Or you can merely make the place a safer and more pleasant home with the simplest lighting setups.

In addition to bringing lights outdoors, you might want to bring an electric outlet outside. Maybe you need it for a lawn mower, for use with portable power tools, to plug in a radio or a broiler. Once you have an outlet, you will find many uses for it. Possibly you will want to use standing lamps on your patio or terrace and plug these lamps into outdoor outlets.

Landscape Lighting

The modern trend toward outdoor living has long held a special challenge for lighting engineers. For years, prohibitive costs have put

1605

1606

garden lighting out of reach of the average homeowner, forcing him indoors after dark. Today, outdoor lighting is within easy reach of the average homeowner.

• To extend the use and enjoyment of property into the night hours.

• To dramatize and beautify the planting and grounds.

• To make it possible to enjoy the fruits of gardening when all the family and guests are together, which is mostly in the evenings.

• To light parking spaces, terraces, paths and steps.

• To augment indoor illumination by lighting up the outside of picture windows, to balance the inside and outside lights, which then cuts out the big black areas of glass, prevents mirror effect, and opens up the outside, making the rooms look much bigger.

• To help keep prowlers away.

KINDS OF FIXTURES

1. The light source of general outside illumination should not be conspicuous.

2. Fixtures during the daytime and at night should blend in with surroundings or be aesthetically an asset.

3. Use standard, commonly available bulbs.

4. Installation should be simple, with the least amount of wiring.

WHAT ARE THE GENERAL PRINCIPLES?

To have effective outdoor illumination, you have to have something to light up, such as; bushes, flowers, rocks, an ornamental wall or fence.

The farther these objects are from the light source, the fainter the illumination will get.

Trees in full leaf, or a solid wall or rock, will illuminate more effectively than bare trees.

Outdoor illumination seen from the inside of a lighted room, requires more wattage, which means more fixtures or bigger lamps than if the same illumination is observed from an unlighted room or dimly lit terrace.

General outdoor illumination needs very little current. One 150-watt flood P.A.R. bulb will illuminate about 1200 square feet of area of trees, 40 feet away, if used in a properly designed fixture. This means that a width of 40′, which is

1607

occupied by trees 30′ to 40′ high, will be satisfactorily illuminated 40′ away. The intensity of this illumination is about that of bright moonlight.

If the same illumination is planned to be viewed from inside a lighted living room, the general illumination outside will have to be raised four or five times in intensity by using four or five 150-watt flood lamps and fixtures instead of one, or using 300-watt flood lamps in half as many fixtures.

How To Place Fixtures

The placing of the fixtures is of primary importance. As a rule fixtures designed for general outdoor illumination will not be conspicuous and will hardly be noticed during daylight because of their design and color and because their size is small compared to the building and the outdoor surroundings. But the story is different with any light source in the evening hours when the fixtures are lighted. Therefore, it is important to know how to place the fixtures. The following are some of the guiding principles:

1. Point the light beam towards the area to be lighted and adjust the position and angle so that direct view of the light source is not visible from any point where people would be disturbed by it. In other words, the fixture should be so located that you never see into it from any place customarily used for walks, or from any part of the house, etc. You see either the back or the side of it. Sometimes, two fixtures will have to be used to accomplish this instead of one.

2. If fixtures are mounted high upon the building, the adjustment is somewhat more difficult, but the effect much more gratifying because it will light up a larger area on account of the higher elevation of the light source.

3. Point the fixtures as close to a horizontal position as possible, without disturbing neighbors, then adjust the side to side horizontal angle as needed.

4. The installation on or near buildings is less costly because no wiring is needed outside the house except the outlets to plug the fixture into.

5. If fixtures are used near the base of buildings, the important thing is to point them away from the direction of walks and from neighbors; also from windows in your own building.

6. If fixtures are used to light the underside of a tree, the higher they are mounted on the trunk the easier it is to conceal the light beam.

7. One of the simplest ways of planning flood lights is in front of bushes with their backs to the picture window.

8. Flood light lamps will give a softer and wider illumination but, for high-lighting, use spot bulbs in the fixtures.

9. For illuminating parking areas, use flood light bulbs. In most cases, one 150-watt lamp will illuminate sufficiently an area of 40'x40'. The light should be placed either high up on the garage and pointed down sufficiently not to blind the drivers, or use low-level diffused lighting fixture. In many cases, sufficient illumination can be obtained by lighting up trees, the garage wall, rocks if any, which would reflect back the light on the parking area or driveway.

Methods of Wiring

Three easy lighting methods—It is possible, of course, to install permanent lighting outdoors. But it is much more flexible, and certainly a simpler beginning, to use one or more of three other methods.

One of these is the weatherproof outlet. Put in several and you can add whatever lights you need at any time, using simple fixtures sold for the purpose. You can install these permanently when you are ready, or you can use them plug-in fashion, putting them away between times.

A second method uses overhead wiring. You can buy what is called weatherproof wire and string it up where you want it. At any point that a light is called for, strip a bit of insulation and tap in with a weatherproof socket. If you want a lot of lights of this type, try to buy a ready-made string of weatherproof sockets like those for Christmas lighting in city shopping districts.

Third, and possibly simplest of the lot, is the porcelain socket

1609

Basic Rules for Outdoor Lighting

Outdoor lighting can be functional or dramatic or both. You can get the most out of outdoor lighting, if you follow these simple rules:

• Don't "lightwash" an area with a single floodlight! It produces a flat and monotonous effect with harsh contrasts and shadows, just the same effect you'd get with a single light when photographing.

• Where possible, place your lights so that they are away from your outdoor relaxation area. Insects are attracted to the lights and it's better to have them far away rather than where you're sitting or eating.

• You can create dramatic lighting effects by using colored lights. Outdoor spotlights are available in color. If you have a fixture that cannot take one of these bulbs, you can buy snap-on colored glass filters to create a colored lighting effect.

• If you are lighting flower beds, use white or green colored lamps. Some flower displays look attractive with yellow.

• Yellow lighting is recommended by manufacturers to keep insects away, or at least not to attract as many insects as white light.

• Generally, blue light should be avoided outdoors. It produces unattractive effects, producing ghost-like appearance for humans and dull effect on grass, shrubs and flowers.

mounted on the side of the house. Screw a swivel socket into it if you need control of the direction of light. Use a reflector bulb—either flood or spot type, depending upon how much area your light is to cover. Any installation like this should be kept well under a roof overhang, because it is not waterproof.

WHICH WIRE TO USE

However you may wish to arrange your outdoor light and power, you'll be working with a few basic essentials. The first of these is wire, because something has to get that current to where you want it and do so without shocking anyone (including the city inspector you may have to deal with in some areas).

First wire or cable you'll need is something to run the circuit from the fusebox, or wherever it now ends, to the point where the outdoor wiring begins. The simplest thing is to use whatever your house is wired with. This may be indoor wire in conduit, steel-armored cable (often called BX), or nonmetallic sheathed cable, such as Romex.

For overhead wiring the standard material is called "weatherproof." It used to come in copper wire only, but now you can get it in aluminum, too—at half the weight and not much more than half the price.

Types of underground cable—For underground installation, the traditional thing is lead-covered cable containing two conductors. Becoming more popular because it is somewhat cheaper, is nonmetallic trench cable; it comes as single wires jacketed in tough neoprene. A non-metallic trench cable containing two wires is also available in some areas. This is somewhat handier to use but is somewhat more expensive.

The size wire you'll use depends upon the circuit to which it is to be hooked. You'll normally tap a 15 ampere circuit, which requires at least No. 14 conductor. If in doubt, you can't go wrong with No. 12.

This applies to all types of wire and cable with one exception. If

Installing an outdoor outlet (at right in drawing) through a wall.

trance ell. At the working end, you'll need a weatherproof outlet and a box to put it into. If you recess the box into a post, use an ordinary switch box such as is used in house wiring. If it isn't to be recessed, get what's called a surface-mount utility box. You'll also need two short pieces of conduit, to protect the wire where it is above ground. Conduit usually comes in 10-foot lengths.

Outdoor Outlet

To install an outdoor outlet, it is necessary to drill through the house wall. It is best to bring the wires from the basement. If you have a concrete or concrete block foundation, drill the hole with a star drill and hammer

you're using weatherproof with an aluminum conductor, go one size larger; use No. 12 for a 15 ampere circuit, No. 10 for a 20 ampere.

Any of the trench cables may be laid in the ground without protection —except in two cases. If you are in an area covered by electrical codes, your code may require putting the cable in conduit. And if there is any likelihood that anyone will dig into the laid cable, it is safer to put it into conduit anyway.

For any part of your wiring that is going to be exposed, use conduit. **You'll find the in-wall type (called E.M.T.)** much easier to use than the heavy conduit, which is similar to water pipe. Just be sure you get fittings for the kind of conduit you are using. Since you probably won't be using wire larger than No. 12, the smallest conduit—½″ diameter—is what you'll want.

INSTALLING AN OUTLET

To install an outdoor plug-in, you'll need fittings for both ends. At the house end, you'll need an en-

The holiday season is a favorite time of the year to light up the outside of your house. Here, outdoor lights are inserted through holes poked in the bottom of colored plastic cups and mounted on a styrofoam backing to make a festive window swag.

Brighten your patio with area lighting. These stoneware lamps (made by the hobbyist-potter owner) are suspended on chains from the house overhang, spotlighting an echeveria in a charming architectural pot.

Lighting at this front entryway provides a warm and safe welcome.

1612

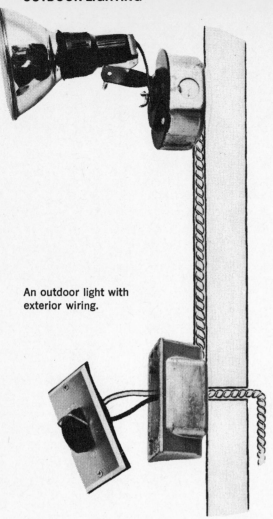

An outdoor light with
exterior wiring.

1614

or a masonry bit with an electric drill. If you go through above the sill, you can use a brace and bit.

Attach a junction box on the inside wall on one side of the hole and a waterproof box on the other side. Run a pipe or conduit through the wall.

Attach a pair of wires to a waterproof outlet set in the outdoor box and run the wires through the pipe or conduit into the junction box inside the house.

Run a pair of wires from a convenient outlet in the basement to the junction box. Join the white wire

from the outlet inside the house to the white wire from the outdoor outlet. Now join the black wires.

Note: always make certain the electricity is *off* when you do any electrical work! Either remove the fuse controlling the line or pull the master switch. See section on *ELECTRICAL WIRING*.

Outdoor Light-Exterior Wiring

There are two ways to attach an outdoor light. The wiring can be run inside the wall or it can be run outside the wall, as illustrated here. This is the easier and quicker way to do the job.

Attach a waterproof box outside a hole that has been drilled through the foundation wall from the basement. If you want, you can add an outdoor type switch to control the light or else place the switch inside the house.

Run a conduit from this outdoor box to the place where the outdoor light will be and attach another waterproof box. You can run several lights off the one line, if you wish. See section on "parallel wiring" under *ELECTRICAL WIRING*.

The wiring inside is similar to that used for an outdoor outlet. On the outside, however, connect a pair of wires to the light and run them to the switch. Connect the black wire from the light to the switch and the black wire from the house to the other end of the switch. The white wire from the house and the white wire from the light are joined together in the waterproof box holding the switch.

Outdoor Light-Interior Wiring

The other method you can use to wire an outdoor light is to bring the necessary cable through the wall—between the exterior siding or brick and the interior wall surfacing material.

This wiring can be done with or without the exterior light switch. If the switch is omitted, then no hole has to be drilled in the wall to connect the switch and a single cable can be used from the basement junction box to the waterproof box holding the outdoor light.

It is necessary to drill through the floor plate or sill to get to the interior cavity between the outer and inner walls. Next, drill a hole for the switch box and another for the wall light.

Use a snake to draw the wire from the outdoor light box to the switch box. Secure the cable so that it does not slip back into the wall opening. Then snake a cable through from the basement junction box to the outdoor switch box.

In wiring, a pair of wires are at-

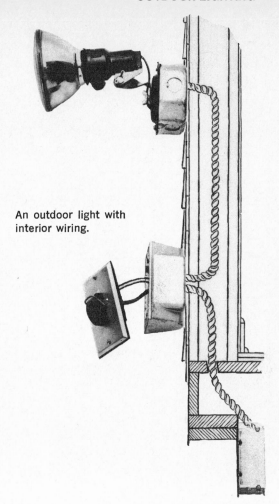

An outdoor light with interior wiring.

Small low-voltage garden lights in a lily-of-the-valley design illuminate the railroad-tie steps leading to the front entrance of this home.

tached to the light fixture. The black wire from the light is joined to one end of the switch and the black wire from inside the house is joined to the other end. The white wire from the light and the white wire from the inside of the house are joined together within the waterproof box housing the outdoor switch.

Lights You Can Use

You have a good choice of individual types of lights and lamps as well as outdoor floodlights. One basic type, for yard and barnyard use, has a reflector and an arm. You fasten it

1615

Fixtures for Outdoor Lighting

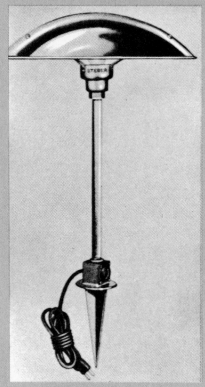
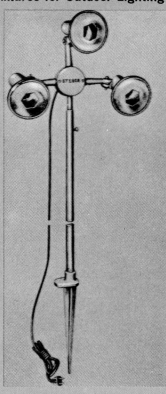
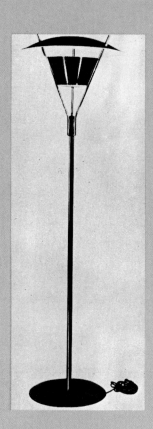

Photographs courtesy of Lightolier, Inc. and Steber Mfg. Co.

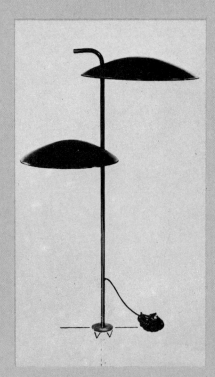
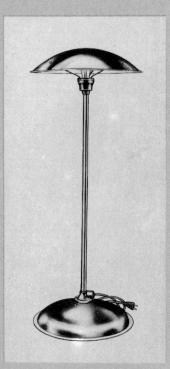
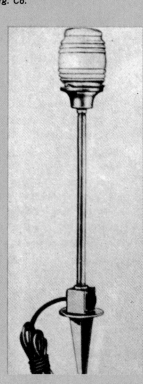

1616

Utilitarian light outside an outbuilding is provided by a simple fixture like this. Conduit serves as the bracket. A switch is placed in easy reach elsewhere, often at the house.

Quickest way to controlled yard lighting is a porcelain socket on the side of house protected by roof. Add swivel and reflector bulb. Mount socket on an octagon box recessed in wall.

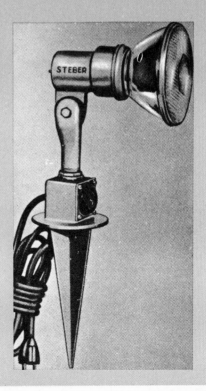

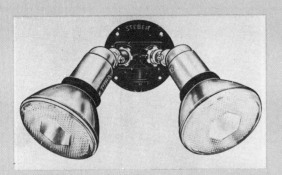

1617

to a wall and screw an ordinary 100- to 200-watt bulb into it. It throws light downward.

Other reflectors, usually offered without arms, surround their bulb and concentrate the light. These also are useful for mounting on a building or post.

For use at ground level, the handiest thing is a unit consisting of socket, base and cord. It can be fastened to a wall if you like or it can be stuck into the ground by means of a spike that comes with it. It is weatherproof when used with the bulb for which it is made: the 150-watt out-

door reflector type, either flood for general lighting or spot for concentrating illumination where you want it.

There's another item you'll get some fun out of—and it will make your outdoor lighting even more spectacular. It's colored glass in a snap-on holder to go with the outdoor reflector bulb. You can get it in red, green, blue or amber.

Garden Outlet

If you want an outlet away from the house, here is one method you can follow. The same technique can

1618

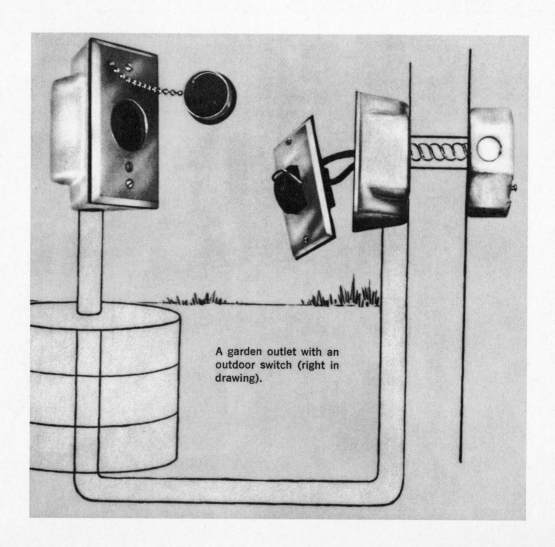

A garden outlet with an outdoor switch (right in drawing).

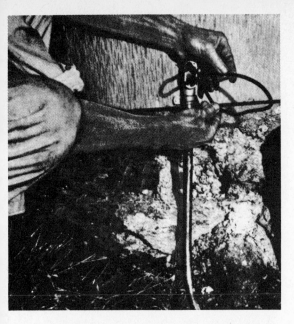

1. Bring current outside with same kind of cable used for the house wiring, lead it through an entrance ell (as shown) and splice it to trench cable. The cable should run through conduit well underground.

2. Run trench cable from entrance ell to point where outlet is wanted. Cable may be put in conduit, or, if the local code permits, buried directly in ground. Taping the cable under a board will protect it.

HOW TO INSTALL AN OUTLET OUTDOORS

3. Cable again enters conduit before emerging from ground. Connect to surface mount box and wire in a weatherproof outlet. Neutral wire should be dabbed with paint or taped for identification.

4. Complete the job by putting on the weathertight cover, which comes with gasket. Spring-loaded cover snaps down to seal outlet against rain when nothing is plugged in.

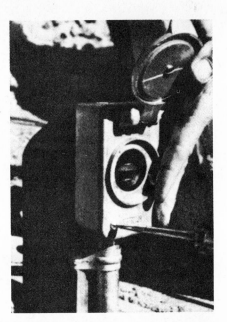

1619

be used for a light, substituting the fixture for the outlet.

An outdoor type of switch and box are mounted on the outside wall of the house and wired in the same manner as the switch used to control an outdoor light mounted on the wall.

An outdoor type of box and outlet are set in a base of concrete anywhere in the yard you wish. The outlet box should be at least 12" above ground level.

The wire from the outlet to the switch box on the wall can be run in a conduit, buried at least 8" below ground level or you can use waterproof trench wire, at least 12" below ground level with a 1x4 board set above the wire to protect it from penetrating garden tools.

The wiring is similar to any outlet and switch combination, but remember to treat the wires coming to the house junction box as if the wires were directly from the fuse box.

1620

An old porch post salvaged from a junk yard makes a handsome support for a yard lamp. The square block originally on top of this one was sawed off and the diameter reduced enough to suit the lamp chosen. To add height, a 36" piece of timber squared to match was added to the bottom of the post, a splint-type joint being used. After a slot ¾" deep had been cut up one side, the cable was wedged in, and the slot puttied full with water-mix filler. Paint, applied after the post was erected, hid the slot. Use enough lead or vinyl cable to reach from the house to the lamp without splicing.

Seen on a house in Colonial Williamsburg, the original of this lantern came from a collection. The homemade version at right is soldered up of tin-can-stock, coathanger wire and an old chandelier fitting. Glass panes should be the frosted kind if bulb is in line of sight.

The wall lamp below is an electrified copy of one on the same house. Its bright tin-plate reflector throws plenty of light. Dull black, bronze or gold stippled on black are all suitable finishes.

Colonial Lights

With street lighting sketchy at best, the colonial home needed gate and porch lamps to light both visitor and homecomer. Today's porch light is a matter of course, but its styling need not be.

If your vacation takes you to Williamsburg, Jamestown, Charlottesville or other historic spots, you'll see many types of house lanterns worth copying. The originals were of course handmade, so they are naturals for the craftsman to duplicate.

You can build good-looking replicas of such antique lamps from tin-can stock, wire and glass. Standard electric fittings bring them up to date, making them as useful as they are ornamental.

1621

1. Cut tin-can stock into 1″ strips. Bend them up to make ½″x½″ angles. Solder together two 6¼″x7″ frames, and join them with 6¼″ pieces, to form the body.

2. Vent holes are 2″ from roof peak and in the center of each side. Hoods to keep rain out are small triangles of tin plate, folded in middle and soldered over holes.

HOW TO MAKE A SQUARE LANTERN

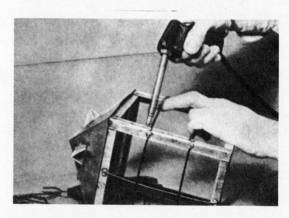

3. To shield glass and further the colonial effect, solder on guards made of coat-hanger wire. File each end bright, hammer flat and use acid flux to solder. Wash all joints well.

4. Base is removable for changing bulb. Make it of twice-folded tin plate. Solder short screws (arrow) into the frame. Drill holes in base. Retain with knurled nuts.

5. Ring fixture, from an old chandelier, screws onto ⅛″ brass pipe soldered into roof. Cord passes down a corner. Insert panes from bottom and solder in clips.

1. Frame for picnic-table light diffuser is a 34″x34″ assembly of 2x2's (actually about 1¾″ square). Corner braces, cut off at 45° angle, measure 13″ on long sides. Assemble with waterproof glue and rust-resistant hardware. Finish with varnish.

2. For octagonal diffuser, use a 26″ square of yellow or rose-colored structural plastic. (This material is most readily available in 26″ widths.) Measure 7⅝″ both ways from each corner, scratch a line between connecting points and cut off the corners.

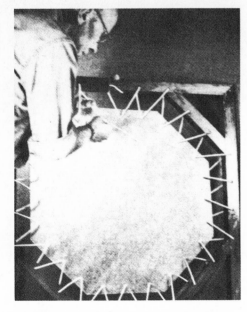

MAKING A LIGHT DIFFUSER

3. Plastic is secured to frame with plastic clothesline. Drill ¼″ holes around plastic and frame; lace in the plastic. Hang the diffuser with more line. Use a plain bulb in a weatherproof socket or—better yet— a weatherproof bulb-socket combination.

1623

Outdoor Storage

Beginning in spring, many families start to move outdoors. First come the garden tools and then the barbecue and accessory items. Outdoor storage is always a problem. Even when there is "extra" room in the garage, there usually isn't enough. If you have a carport, chances are you are really cramped for outdoor storage space.

Here are several projects, outdoor built-ins, to solve that storage problem. Also see sections on *CARPORT* and *GARAGE*.

Outdoor Storage Wall

Here is an attractive outdoor-built-in that is as useful as it is good looking. It provides plenty of space for storing garden tools, fertilizers, children's toys and barbecue equipment. Furthermore, it has handy shelf space for pots and plants. In the summer, the table-door can be folded down for summer dining or garden center work.

This unit can be built free-standing or attached to the house or garage as illustrated. Either way, you will add 336 cubic feet of storage space.

1624

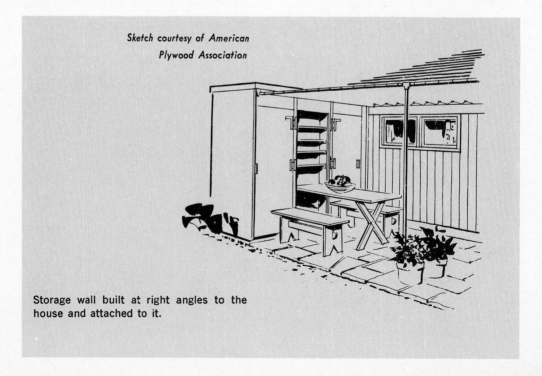

Sketch courtesy of American Plywood Association

Storage wall built at right angles to the house and attached to it.

Storage wall combined with a covered patio and a woven plywood fence. See section on **Fences** for how-to details for the woven fence.

Storage wall at the back of the garage.

Basic construction details showing the over-all measurements and position of the major parts of the basic frame.

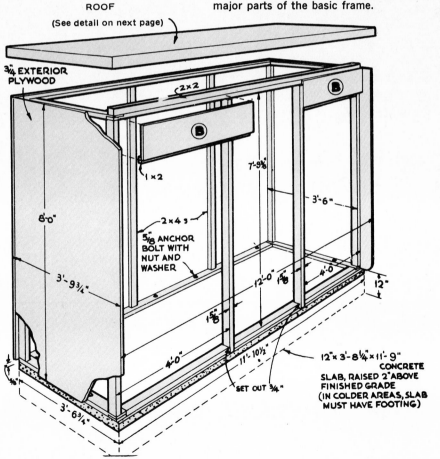

ROOF

(See detail on next page)

3¾" EXTERIOR PLYWOOD

2 × 2

B

B

1 × 2

7'-9⅜"

3'-6"

8'-0"

2 × 4 s

⅝" ANCHOR BOLT WITH NUT AND WASHER

3'- 9¾"

12'-0" ⅝

4'-0

12"

⅝

4'-0"

11'- 10½"

SET OUT ¾"

3'- 6¾"

12"× 3'-8½"×11'-9"
CONCRETE SLAB, RAISED 2" ABOVE FINISHED GRADE (IN COLDER AREAS, SLAB MUST HAVE FOOTING)

1625

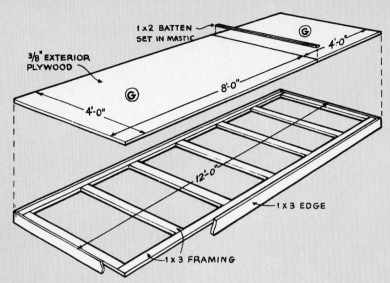

1 x 2 BATTEN
SET IN MASTIC

3/8" EXTERIOR PLYWOOD

4'-0"

8'-0"

4'-0"

G

G

12'-0"

1 X 3 EDGE

1 x 3 FRAMING

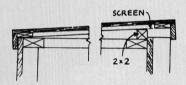

SCREEN

2 x 2

Detailed view of construction of the roof, showing the 1x3 framing, 1x3 edge and 3/8" fir plywood top.

Section view through top and roof. Note that 2x2 is placed on top of 2x4 plate to allow for slope permitting drainage.

Detail showing the end panel. The 2x4's may be nailed to the plywood panel before placing on the 2x4 sole.

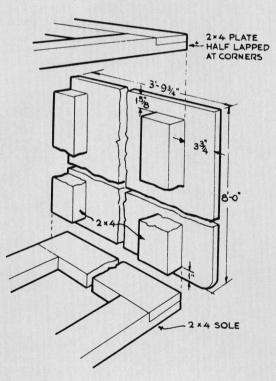

2 x 4 PLATE
HALF LAPPED AT CORNERS

3'-9 3/4"

1 5/8"

3 3/4"

8'-0"

2 x 4

2 x 4 SOLE

How to make the slide for the table top.

1626

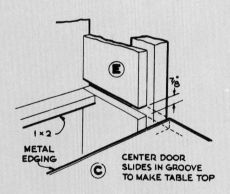

E

7/8"

1 x 2

METAL EDGING

C

CENTER DOOR SLIDES IN GROOVE TO MAKE TABLE TOP

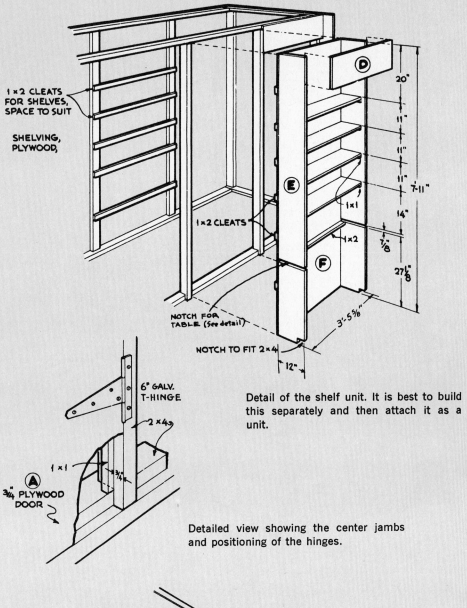

1 x 2 CLEATS FOR SHELVES, SPACE TO SUIT

SHELVING, PLYWOOD,

1 x 2 CLEATS

NOTCH FOR TABLE (See detail)

NOTCH TO FIT 2 x 4

20"

11"

11"

11"

7-11"

14"

7/8"

27⅛"

1 x 1

1 x 2

3'-5⅝"

12"

6" GALV. T-HINGE

2 x 4s

1 x 1

¾"

A

¾" PLYWOOD DOOR

Detail of the shelf unit. It is best to build this separately and then attach it as a unit.

Detailed view showing the center jambs and positioning of the hinges.

1627

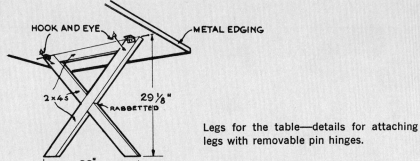

HOOK AND EYE

METAL EDGING

2 x 4s RABBETTED

29⅛"

30"

Legs for the table—details for attaching legs with removable pin hinges.

View of the outdoor storage wall closed and open.

1628

Materials Needed		
FIR PLYWOOD		
NUMBER OF PANELS	**SIZE**	**EXTERIOR GRADE**
5	4'x8'x¾"	A-C
4	4'x8'x¾"	A-A
3	4'x8'x⅜"	A-C

LUMBER	
SIZE	**NUMBER OF FEET**
2x4	136
1x3	84
1x2	60
1x1	22
2x2	12

HARDWARE*
Six 6" T-hinges   Six hooks and eyes
Ten ⅝" anchor bolts with nuts and washers
* All exposed hardware should be galvanized

MISCELLANEOUS
Concrete base for slab. See sections on **Concrete** and **Foundations.**

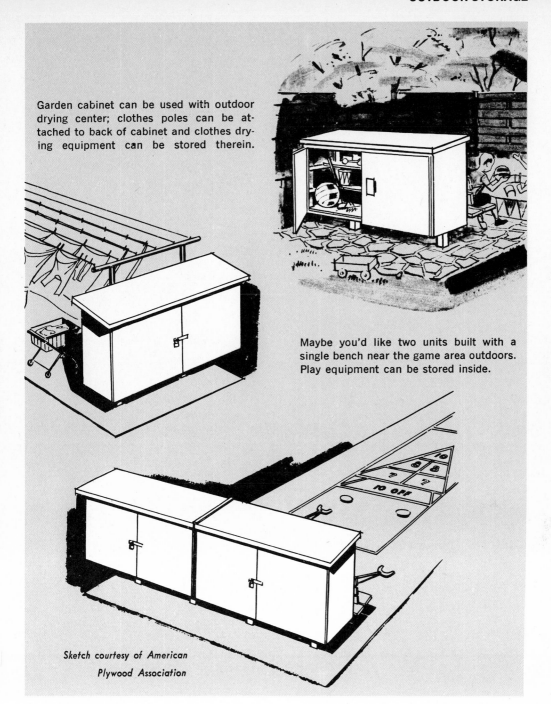

Garden cabinet can be used with outdoor drying center; clothes poles can be attached to back of cabinet and clothes drying equipment can be stored therein.

Maybe you'd like two units built with a single bench near the game area outdoors. Play equipment can be stored inside.

Sketch courtesy of American Plywood Association

1629

Garden Storage Cabinet

This handy all-purpose outdoor storage locker can be used in a dozen ways around your home. Use it near the children's play area for toys and games . . . next to your outdoor fireplace to hold barbecue equipment. The cabinet can be built with a bench attached or may be made without it.

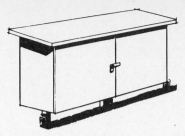

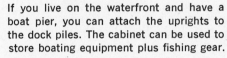

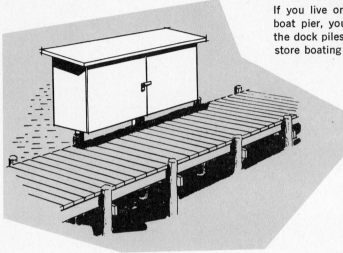

If you live on the waterfront and have a boat pier, you can attach the uprights to the dock piles. The cabinet can be used to store boating equipment plus fishing gear.

1630

Materials Needed		
FIR PLYWOOD		
NUMBER OF PANELS	SIZE	EXTERIOR GRADE
2	4′x8′x¾″	A-C
1	4′x8′x¾″	A-A
1	4′x8′x⅜″	A-C
LUMBER		
SIZE	FEET NEEDED	WHERE USED
2x4	80	Framework
1x3	60	Framework
4x4	16	Supporting posts
HARDWARE*		
3 pairs of 2½″ tight-pin butt hinges 1 pair of 4½″ safety hinge hasps 1 pair of hook and eye * All exposed hardware should be galvanized		
MISCELLANEOUS		
Concrete for the base. See sections on **Concrete** and **Foundations.**		

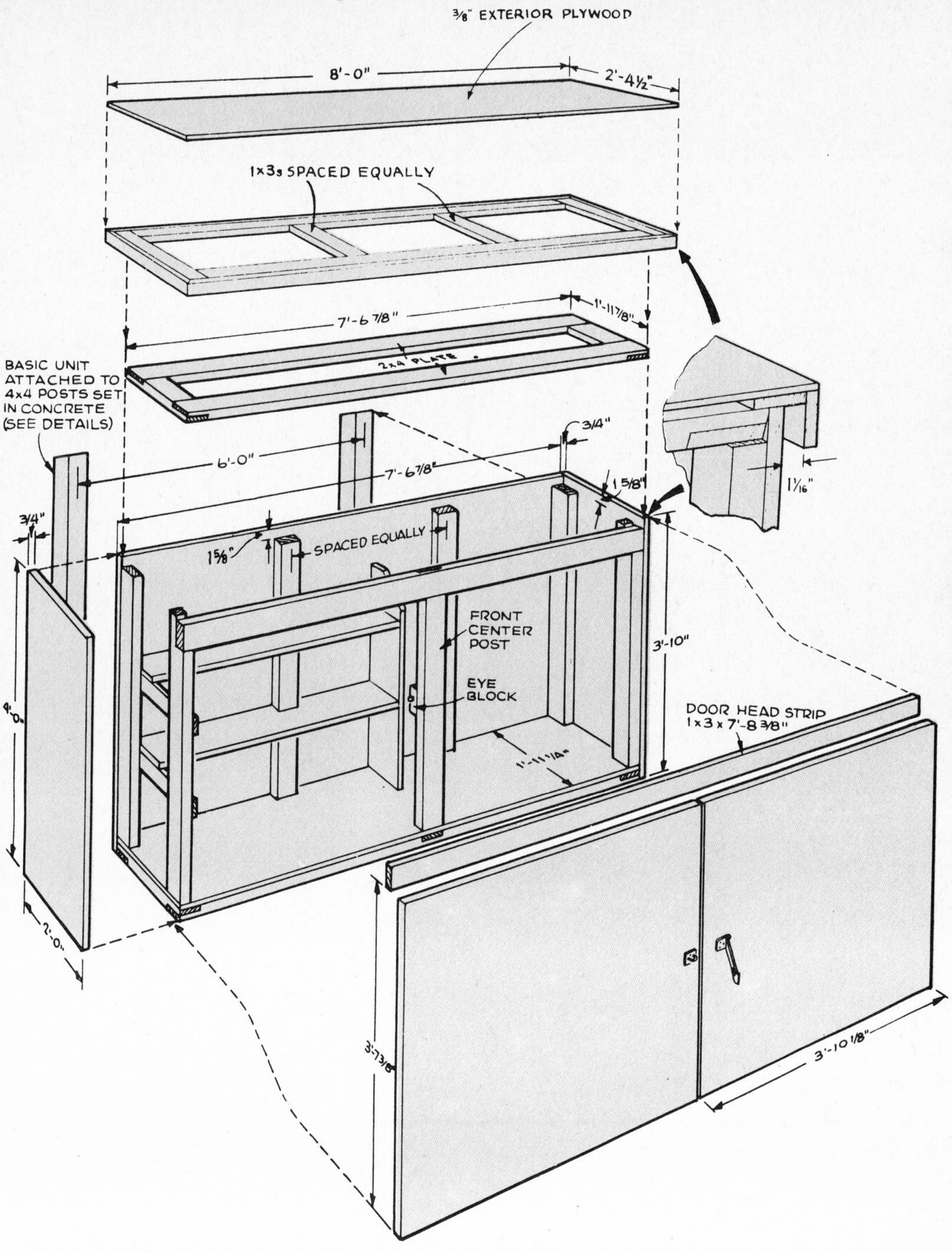
3/8" EXTERIOR PLYWOOD
8'-0"
2'-4½"
1×3s SPACED EQUALLY
7'-6 7/8"
1'-11⅞"
2x4 PLATE
BASIC UNIT
ATTACHED TO
4x4 POSTS SET
IN CONCRETE
(SEE DETAILS)
3/4"
6'-0"
7'-6⅞"
1⅝"
1⅝"
SPACED EQUALLY
3/4"
1 1/16"
FRONT
CENTER
POST
EYE
BLOCK
3'-10"
4'-0"
1'-11¼"
DOOR HEAD STRIP
1x3 x 7'-8⅜"
2'-0"
3'-7⅜"
3'-10⅛"

Pulled apart diagram to show construction details. Over-all dimensions of the unit: top—⅜" plywood panel 8'x2'4½"; box without the top—4' high at peak, 3'10" high at low side and 7'8⅜" wide and 2'¾" from back to front. Note: the height of the entire assembly mounted can be variable depending upon the height of the posts above the ground. If you add a bench to the cabinet, then the top of the bench should be about 15" above ground.

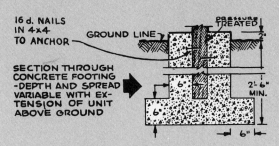

16 d. NAILS IN 4x4 TO ANCHOR

GROUND LINE

PRESSURE TREATED

SECTION THROUGH CONCRETE FOOTING -DEPTH AND SPREAD VARIABLE WITH EXTENSION OF UNIT ABOVE GROUND

2"

2'-6" MIN.

6"

Detail for footing at each post. See sections on **Concrete** and **Foundations** for how-to.

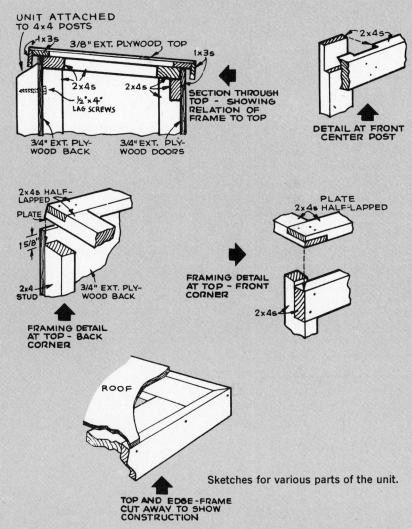

UNIT ATTACHED TO 4x4 POSTS

1x3s

3/8" EXT. PLYWOOD, TOP

1x3s

2x4s

2x4s

1/2" x 4" LAG SCREWS

3/4" EXT. PLYWOOD BACK

3/4" EXT. PLYWOOD DOORS

SECTION THROUGH TOP - SHOWING RELATION OF FRAME TO TOP

2x4s

DETAIL AT FRONT CENTER POST

2x4s HALF-LAPPED

PLATE

1 5/8"

2x4 STUD

3/4" EXT. PLYWOOD BACK

FRAMING DETAIL AT TOP - BACK CORNER

PLATE

2x4s HALF-LAPPED

FRAMING DETAIL AT TOP - FRONT CORNER

2x4s

ROOF

TOP AND EDGE-FRAME CUT AWAY TO SHOW CONSTRUCTION

Sketches for various parts of the unit.

1632

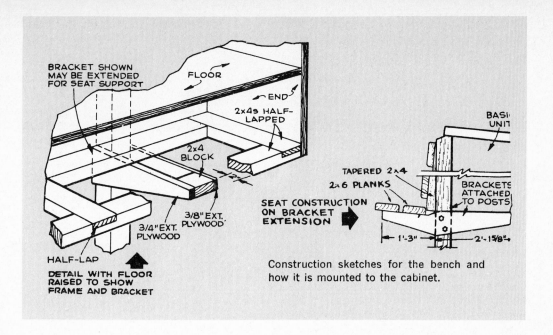

BRACKET SHOWN
MAY BE EXTENDED
FOR SEAT SUPPORT

FLOOR

END

2x4s HALF-
LAPPED

2x4
BLOCK

3/8" EXT.
PLYWOOD

3/4" EXT.
PLYWOOD

HALF-LAP

DETAIL WITH FLOOR
RAISED TO SHOW
FRAME AND BRACKET

TAPERED 2x4

2x6 PLANKS

SEAT CONSTRUCTION
ON BRACKET
EXTENSION

BASIC
UNIT

BRACKETS
ATTACHED
TO POSTS

1'-3"   2'-15/8"

Construction sketches for the bench and
how it is mounted to the cabinet.

Storage Port

While this roomy storage port is designed to hold everything from the family car to a trowel, it can be built as individual cabinets without providing for the overhead covering for the car. The gardenside closet is big enough to hold a wheelbarrow and fertilizer. Smaller cabinets can be used for tools and cleaning equipment, while the bigger cabinets are large enough to hold a bicycle and refuse cans.

For step-by-step construction details, see *CARPORT*.

1633

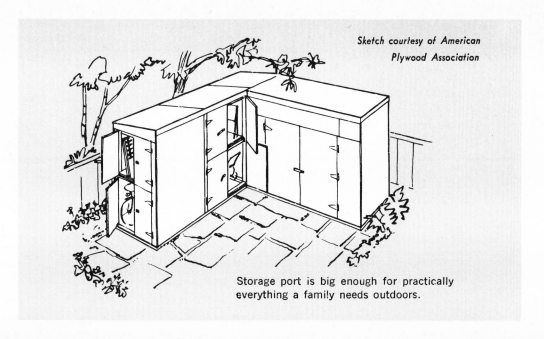

Sketch courtesy of American Plywood Association

Storage port is big enough for practically everything a family needs outdoors.

Garbage Hideaway

Like it or not, your garbage cans do present a storage problem. Here's one way to solve that problem of where to put them and how to move them. The hideaway is built from a single sheet of plywood. It holds two standard-size garbage cans and is light enough to be moved anywhere. The plywood-and-lumber cart is ideal for moving the cans up and down the driveway, and is also sturdy enough to transport bags of fertilizer and grass seed.

The Screen

The garbage can screen is a simple project that you should be able to complete in about 3 hours. You'll need one 4'x8' sheet of ¾" Ext. DFPA grade-trademarked rough-sawn plywood siding; two 2x4x12'; one 2x2x12'; two 2x2x8'; one 2x2x7'; three 1x4x8'; 4 corner angles; galvanized screws and nails (see drawing).

1634

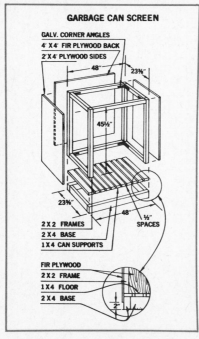

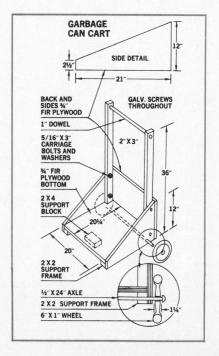

Cut the 2x4 into two 45″ and two 23⅜″ lengths; the 2x2s into four 45¾″, three 45″ and four 20⅜″ lengths; and the 1x4 into twelve 23⅜″ lengths. From the plywood, cut a 4′x4′ back and two 2′x4′ sides. Assemble as in the drawing, then finish with water-repellent stain.

The Cart

You should be able to build the garbage can cart in 2 to 3 hours. These are the materials you'll need: ¾″ A-B Ext. DFPA grade-trademarked plywood, one 20″ x 20¼″, one 12″ x 21½″, one 14½″ x 21″; one 2x3x6′; one 2x2x4′; 2′ of 1″ dowel; ½″ x 24″ axle (look in the Sears catalog if your local hardware store can't supply this); two 6″ x 1″ wheels (same source); four ⁵⁄₁₆″ x 3″ carriage bolts, nuts, washers; 1¼″ galvanized screws.

Cut the 14½″ x 21″ plywood diagonally for sides (see detail). Cut two 33¾″ 2x3s; use the leftover piece for a support block under the cart. Cut two 20¼″ 2x2s. Assemble the cart as in the drawing. Finish with water-repellent stain.

Modular Storage Units

Make even part of this project and you'll agree that outdoor storage was never so practical, versatile and economical. Even with one modular unit (approximately 4′ x 4′ x 8′), you'll have a complete storage center for your patio or garden. Or build several units for all the storage space you want — all the accessories you want them to hold.

Two basic units are all you need to support the optional accessories (not all at the same time): a picnic table and bench, or work surface between storage units, or a peaked roof. For the kids, a monkey bar/ladder, a roof to crawl through, and a climb-through bench. Add one or more of these accessories — any time. Arrange and rearrange the basic units and accessories any way you want. On casters, mobility is easy. Or mount the units on a concrete base for permanence. And if you move, take everything along. The basic units are assembled with bolts and wing nuts, so they're easily demountable.

The accessories that permit this kind of flexibility are designed to fit into slots cut into the backs of the basic units, and/or into connectors that may be bolted to the sides of each basic unit. A standard lean-to greenhouse as shown may also be used in conjunction with these storage units.

This fresh approach to modular outdoor storage is designed well within the capabilities of a home handyman with some experience in woodworking. The project can be built with plywood, lumber, hardware, and a set of hand tools. A conventional brace, bit, coping saw and keyhole saw will handle the curved cuts. However, a few basic power tools like a drill, table, or portable saw and sabre saw will greatly simplify the job. A router would also come in handy.

Before starting, study the plans thoroughly and check through each construction step so all the details are clearly in mind. Note that the photos merely illustrate the general appearance of the units; for complete accuracy, refer only to the plans.

1635

The Basic Module

First lay out the plywood panels for cutting as shown in cutting diagrams. Use a straightedge and carpenter's square for accuracy. Remember to allow for saw kerfs when plotting the dimensions. If in doubt, check the width of your saw cut. Cut out pieces and true the edges with a coarse sanding block. Fill exposed plywood edges and any face defects with natural paste wood filler. Allow to dry, then sand smooth.

Glue and nail the 2 x 2 frame assembly on both side panels, back panel and front panel of the module. Glue and nail the 4 x 4 foundation as well. The optional shelf or peg supports may also be installed and drilled for pegs at this point.

Round sharp corners slightly with a sanding block, and clean MDO plywood surfaces with a tack cloth to prepare for painting. Select a good quality paint and stain, and finish all exterior surfaces. Different colors on varying sections give a bright, colorful effect.

When paint is thoroughly dry, begin assembly of the unit. (During assembly, use mastic at all basic joints.) Set both side panels on edge with the back facing up and lightly clamp the plywood base and roof to the side panels. Drill ¼″ bolt holes through the base and roof panels and framing members. Fasten the roof to the sides with wing nuts and bolts. Then lay the back panel in place, and drill bolt holes through the back panel and insert bolts. At this point, drill bolt holes into roof and base, through framing members of the back panel, and insert bolts through

the roof holes. Then turn the unit on its back, lay the front panel in place and drill through the roof and framing members of front panel. Insert bolts through new holes in the roof panel and secure with wing nuts. Also drill holes through front panel and side framing members; insert bolts and secure with wing nuts, but remove the base entirely. Nail-glue the plywood base to the 4 x 4 foundation. Using the pilot holes in the plywood base, drill through the foundation. (If a concrete foundation is desired, see drawing; otherwise proceed as follows.) Countersink bolt holes in the bottom of the foundation, insert six-inch carriage bolts, and set the side panels with roof onto the foundation assembly. Fasten all parts of module with wing nuts. (Casters may also be fastened to the 4 x 4 foundation; see drawing for details.)

Apply the piano hinge, door catch, lock (optional), and handle to the door. While a plywood door handle adds an interesting visual touch, standard door hardware will work as well and may be easier to install. Finally, hang the door in place. Add shelves (see "accessories" below for size) and pegs as desired. Recommended minimum peg length is four inches.

If more than one module will be built and accessories will be used, drill holes for connectors (see "accessories" below for details.) Connector installation can be made any time with bolts. The greenhouse shown may also be installed, which requires adjustment of the greenhouse base to equalize the height between the storage unit and roof of the lean-to. If the greenhouse is off-

1640

set as shown, a back wall of plywood must be provided, the length depending on the area exposed by the offset. The width of the door that would open inside the greenhouse should also be reduced by about half to prevent the top of the door from striking the greenhouse roof.

Accessories

Decide on the accessories you want to make. For all accessories, cut dowels to length. If 2 ⅝″ dowels are not available, and 3 x 3 finished lumber is used, see drawing for "rounding" details. Next, lay out plywood panels and cut out pieces. Then sand edges, slightly rounding corners, and fill exposed edge defects. Sand smooth when dry.

For all dowels except those in monkey bar/ladder accessory, measure in from ends as shown and crosscut ¾-inch deep at marks. Saw lengthwise between crosscuts as shown for the particular accessory you are making to form a flat surface. Also, predrill all round plywood end caps for screw holes.

Flat Roof

Glue-nail ends of plywood roof onto dowels. Then glue each long edge of plywood roof, and slip holes of plywood end beams over dowels. Nail end beams onto roof edges. Screw the plywood caps onto glued dowel ends as shown.

Peaked Roof

Hinge plywood roof ends together. Pre-drill screw holes at each end of hinged roof, pre-drilling flattened

THE BASIC MODULE

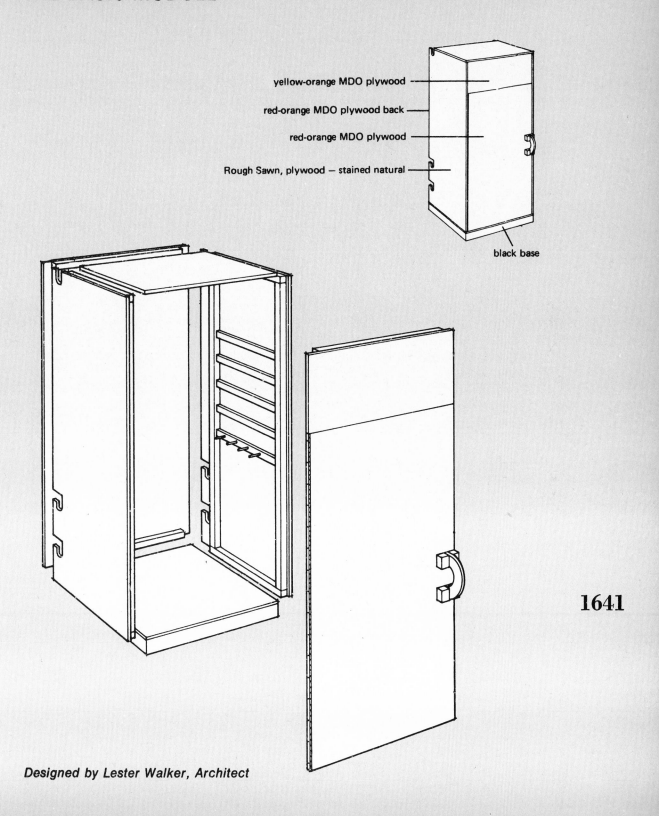

yellow-orange MDO plywood

red-orange MDO plywood back

red-orange MDO plywood

Rough Sawn, plywood — stained natural

black base

1641

Designed by Lester Walker, Architect

OUTDOOR STORAGE

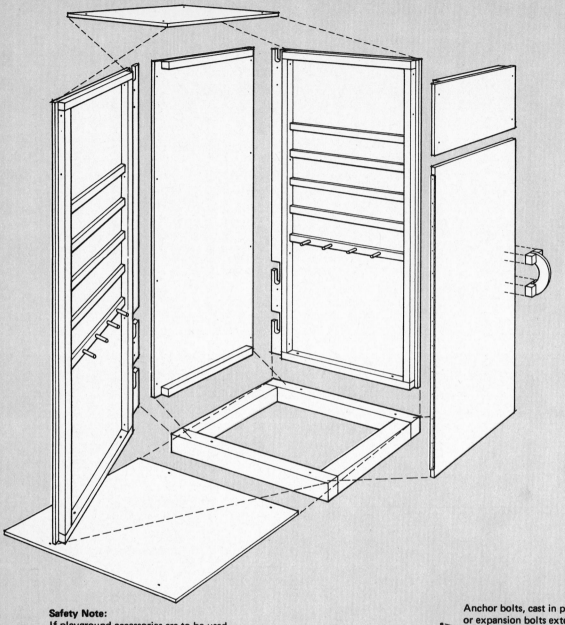

Safety Note:
If playground accessories are to be used, modules should be permanently mounted on concrete foundations.

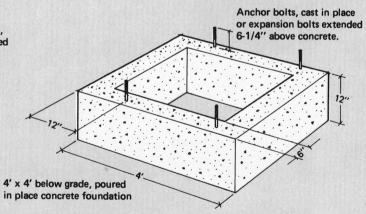

Anchor bolts, cast in place or expansion bolts extended 6-1/4'' above concrete.

12''

12''

6''

4'

4' x 4' below grade, poured in place concrete foundation

MATERIALS LIST

Unfinished average cost of one module: app. $75.00. Cost does not include optional items, and varies regionally across the country. Quantities and material grades purchased will also affect cost.

PLYWOOD

QTY.	SIZE	PLYWOOD GRADE	USE
1 panel	3/4" x 4' x 8'	EXT-DFPA A-C	Roof & base
2 panels	3/4" x 4' x 8'	EXT-DFPA MDO	Front & back
2 panels	5/8" x 4' x 8'	EXT-DFPA ROUGH SAWN	Sides

NOTE: For side panels, any Exterior Type DFPA textured or non-textured plywood may be used. However, if side panel plywood thickness other than 5/8" is used, be sure to adjust drawing dimensions accordingly. EXT-DFPA A-C plywood, which has the structural strength of MDO (Medium Density Overlaid), but not the smooth, ideal surface for paint, may be substituted for MDO plywood at a cost reduction of about 50% per panel. Shelves and handle can be made of excess plywood from accessories' material (see cutting diagram for accessories). If accessories are not built, an additional panel of EXT-DFPA MDO 3/4" x 4' x 8' plywood will yield more than 5 recommended shelves and door handle.

LUMBER

QUANTITY	SIZE	USE
16 lin. ft.	4" x 4"	Foundation
60 lin. ft.	2" x 2"	Framing and door handle blocks
40 lin. ft.	1" x 2"	Shelf rests
4 ft. dowel (or length as needed)	1/2" dia.	Shelf pegs

HARDWARE

QTY.	ITEM	SIZE	USE
1 box	Galv. finish nails	6d	Framing
8 ea.	Galv. common nails	16d	Foundation
20 ea.	Galv. carriage bolts and wing nuts	1/4" x 2-3/4"	Assembly
6 ea.	Galv. carriage bolts and wing nuts	1/4" x 6"	Foundation assembly
2 ea.	Galv. carriage bolts, washers and nuts	3/16" x 4"	Door handle
8 ea.	Galv. flat head screws	#10 1-1/2"	Door handle
1 ea.	Piano hinge	6'	Module door
1 box	Brass flat head screws	#4 3/4"	Piano hinge
1 ea.	Door catch		Door catch

MISCELLANEOUS

Surface putty for filling core gap holes, caulking compound, waterproof glue, as needed. Paint and stain as needed. Optional castors or concrete base as desired (see drawing for material requirements).

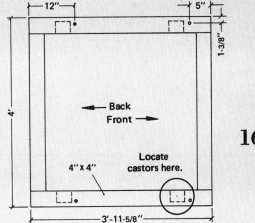

1643

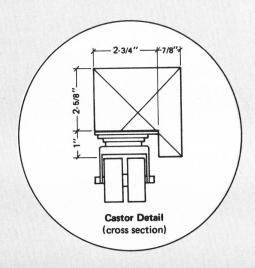

Castor Detail
(cross section)

Left Side Panel

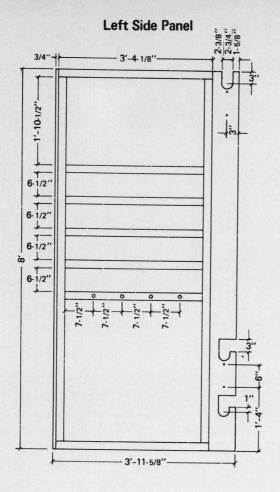

Back

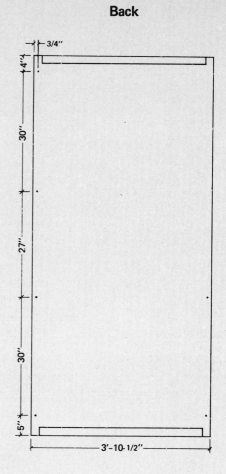

1644

Bottom

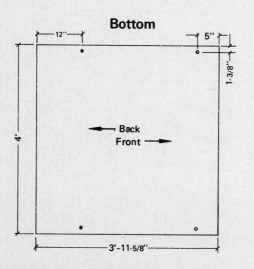

Top

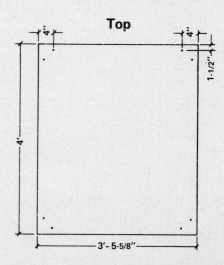

Right Side Panel

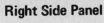
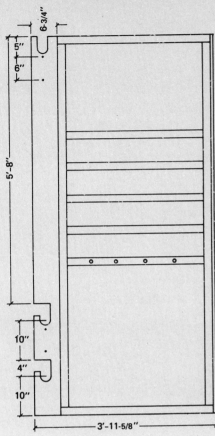

Door

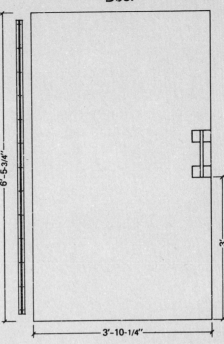

Front

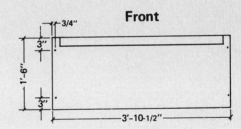

Door Handle

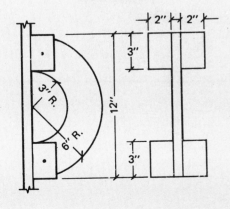

Foundation

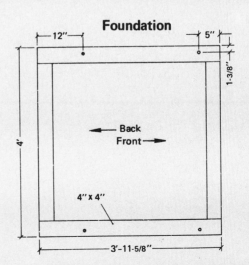

1645

PANEL LAYOUT

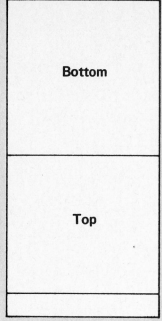

EXT-DFPA A-C plywood,
3/4'' x 4' x 8'

EXT-DFPA
Rough Sawn plywood,
5/8'' x 4' x 8'

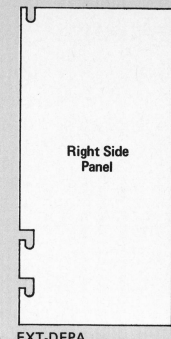

EXT-DFPA
Rough Sawn plywood,
5/8'' x 4' x 8'

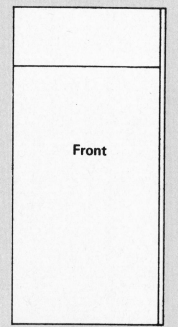

EXT-DFPA
MDO plywood,
3/4'' x 4' x 8'

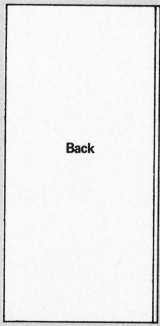

EXT-DFPA
MDO plywood,
3/4'' x 4' x 8'

1646

ACCESSORIES

FLAT ROOF ASSEMBLY

red-orange (all parts)

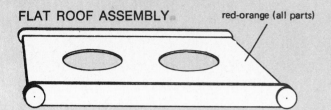

SHELVES

BENCH ASSEMBLY

red-orange (all parts)

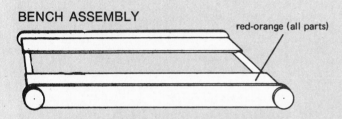

CONNECTORS

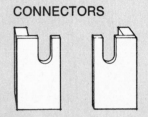

TABLE ASSEMBLY

red-orange (all parts)

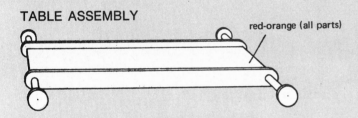

PEAKED ROOF ASSEMBLY

red-orange (all parts)

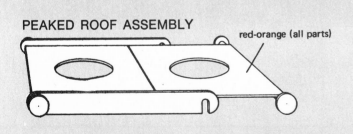

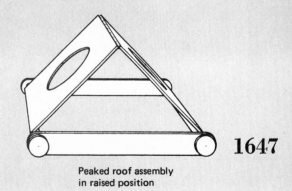

1647

Peaked roof assembly
in raised position

MONKEY BAR/LADDER ASSEMBLY

red-orange (all parts)

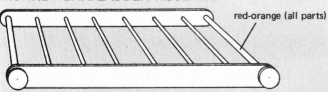

MATERIALS LIST

Unfinished average cost of all accessories: app. $109.00. Cost varies regionally across the country. Quantities and material grades purchased will also affect cost.

The following list is based on the construction requirements of all accessories, since material economies can best be obtained this way. However, if you do not choose to make all the accessories, determine your material requirements from the drawing of the accessory you plan to build.

PLYWOOD

QUANTITY	SIZE	PLYWOOD GRADE	USE
5 panels	3/4" x 4' x 8'	EXT-DFPA MDO	Parts

LUMBER

QUANTITY	SIZE	USE
12 lin. ft.	2" x 4"	Connector cleats (12)
40-1/2 ft. dowel	2-5/8" dia.	End supports
22-1/2 ft. dowel	1-5/8" dia.	Monkey Bar/Ladder

NOTE: If 2-5/8" dia. dowel is not available, order a good grade of 3" x 3" finished lumber (actual 2-5/8") and round corners as shown in drawing.

HARDWARE

QTY.	ITEM	SIZE	USE
1 box	Galv. flat head screws	#10 2-1/2"	Secure end caps to 2-5/8" dowels, side beams to monkey bar/ladder dowels, peaked roof to dowels, and plywood connector to 2" x 4" cleat.
1 ea.	Piano hinge	4'	Peaked roof
1 box	Brass flat head screws	#4 3/4"	Piano hinge
8 ea. (2 per connector)	Galv. carriage bolts and wing nuts	1/4" x 2-3/4"	Secure connector cleat to module

MISCELLANEOUS

Rope on peaked roof is optional; order 8' of 1/2" nylon rope, 2 eye bolts, 4 nuts and 4 washers. Order surface putty, waterproof glue and paint as needed.

SHELVES AND CONNECTORS

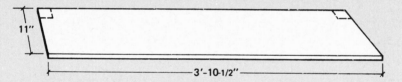

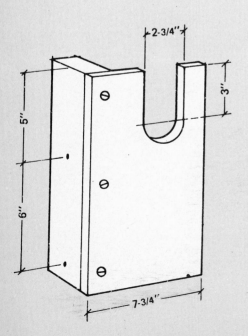

Five shelves per module are recommended. Since shelves are optional, you may want more, less, or none at all, depending on your storage requirements. Notch corners of shelves to fit around framing at back of module.

Connectors are required if modules are not placed back to back and you wish to attach accessories. Determine the number of connectors you need by considering the number of modules you plan to build and the module arrangements you may use. For instance, if two modules are placed side by side with accessories between, 12 connectors may be required.

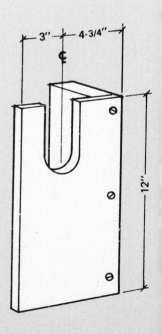

FLAT ROOF

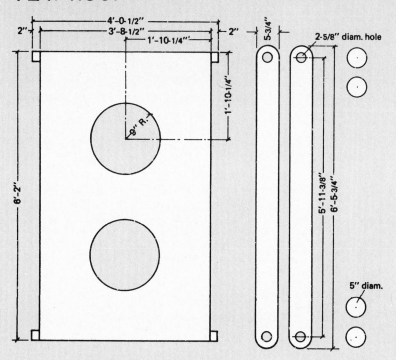

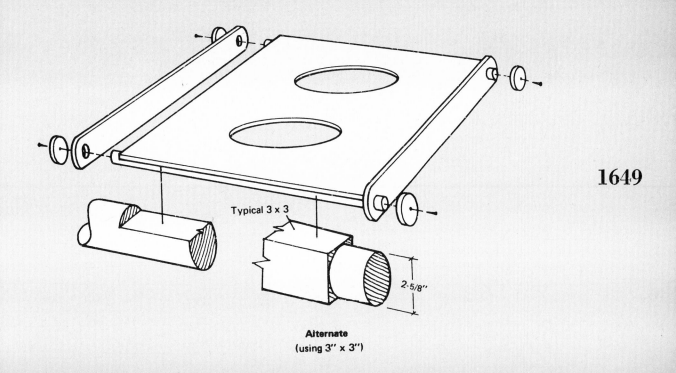

1649

Alternate
(using 3" x 3")

PEAKED ROOF

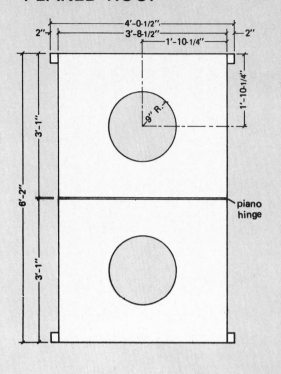

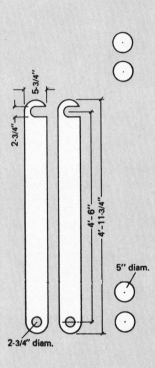

1650

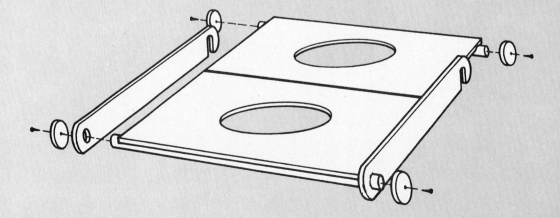

TABLE

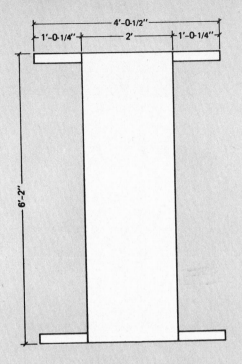

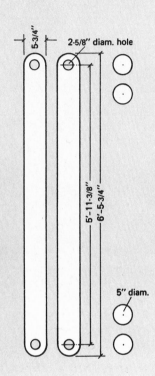

1651

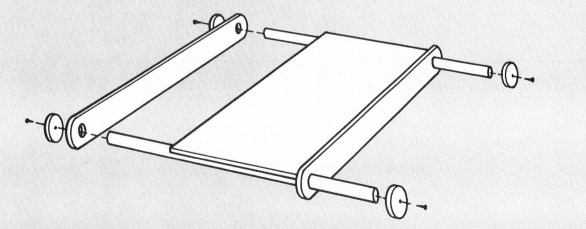

BENCHES

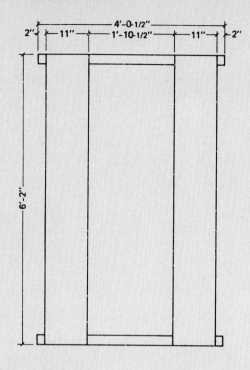

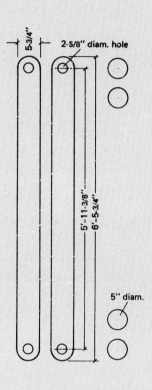

1652

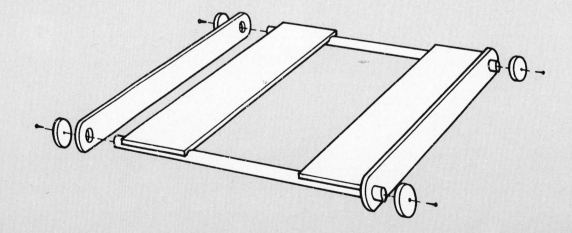

MONKEY BAR/LADDER

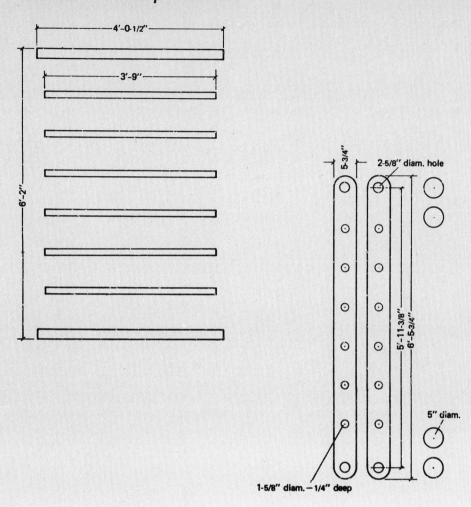

1653

PANEL LAYOUT 5 Panels: EXT-DFPA Medium Density Overlaid plywood, 3/4'' x 4' x 8'

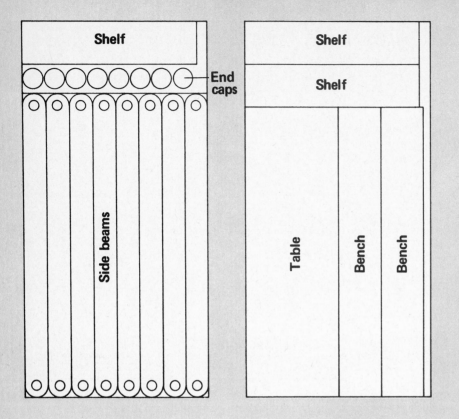

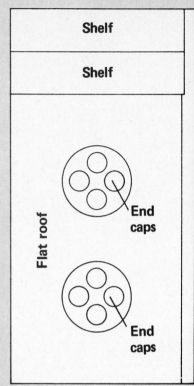

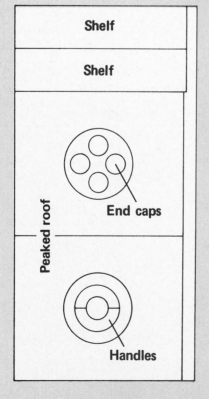

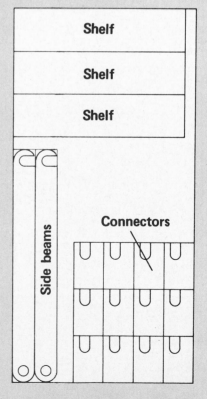

1654

CLUSTER ARRANGEMENTS

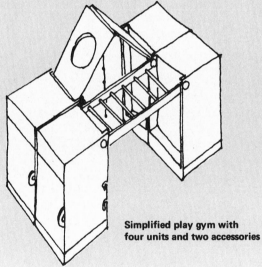

Storage module/picnic table combination — note two modules are necessary for accessory use

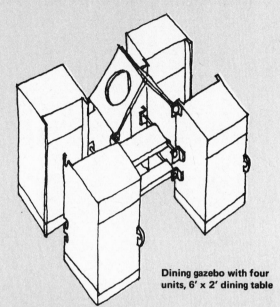

Dining gazebo with four units, 6' x 2' dining table

Simplified play gym with four units and two accessories

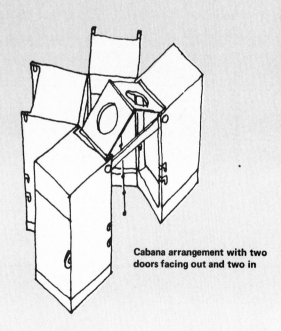

Cabana arrangement with two doors facing out and two in

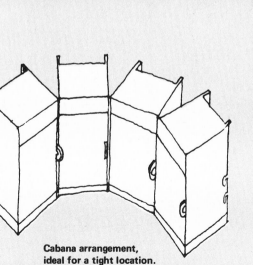

Cabana arrangement, ideal for a tight location.

(Cont. p. 1656)

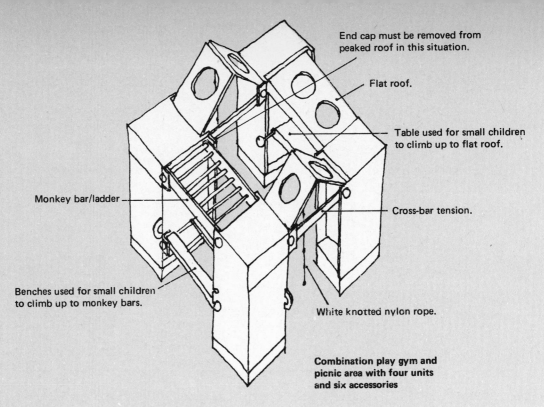

End cap must be removed from peaked roof in this situation.

Flat roof.

Table used for small children to climb up to flat roof.

Monkey bar/ladder

Cross-bar tension.

Benches used for small children to climb up to monkey bars.

White knotted nylon rope.

Combination play gym and picnic area with four units and six accessories

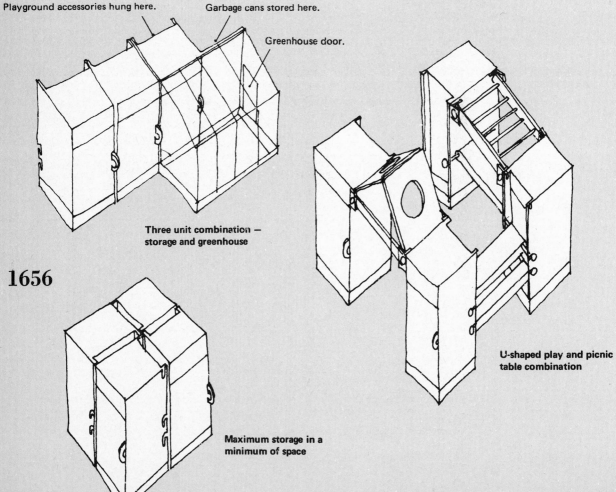

Playground accessories hung here.

Garbage cans stored here.

Greenhouse door.

Three unit combination — storage and greenhouse

1656

Maximum storage in a minimum of space

U-shaped play and picnic table combination

dowel at the same time. Then glue ends of plywood roof and fasten roof panel ends to dowels with screws. Nails may be substituted for screws in plywood-dowel connection if children will not be climbing on roof. (Optional: secure eye bolts in roof to hold nylon rope for children to climb.) Slip holes of plywood end beam connectors over ends of dowel as shown. Screw the plywood caps onto glued dowel ends.

Table

See drawing. Basic instructions are the same as for "Flat Roof" assembly.

Benches

Glue-nail ends of plywood onto dowels. Then glue outside edges of each plywood bench. Slip holes of plywood end beams onto bench edges. Screw the plywood caps onto glued dowel ends as shown.

Monkey Bar/Ladder

Along the center of each end beam, mark evenly spaced locations for each 1⅝" dowel, and drill 1⅝" diameter holes (¼" deep) into one side of each beam. Glue 1 ⅝" dowel ends, insert into end beams and pre-drill the opposite side of end beams for screws. By pre-drilling (offcenter) into each dowel, the dowel is less apt to rotate in use. Then slip the 2 ⅝" dowels through holes in each end beam. Glue these dowel ends, and screw the plywood caps onto the dowel ends as shown.

Shelves and Connectors

Five shelves per module are recommended. Since shelves are optional, you may want more, less, or none at all, depending on your storage requirements.

Note: Notch corners of shelves to fit around framing at back of module.

Connectors are required if modules are not placed back to back and you wish to attach accessories. Determine the number of connectors you need by considering the number of modules you plan to build and the module arrangements you may use. For instance, if two modules are placed side by side with accessories between, 12 connectors may be required.

Paint and Painting

Amateur house painters never had as much help as today. Scores of new paints and equipment placed on the market in the last few years make it possible for the weekend handyman to paint his own house almost as easily as a professional. From one-coat paints to disposable blowtorches, everything has been designed to make the job go faster, look better and cost less.

With the new outside rollers, you can paint an average-size house in a couple of days. Add an extension handle and you can roll a terrace without stooping down, reach a roof without leaving the ground. Specialized aids with built-in know-how tackle the hard spots for you.

Better still, you don't have to spend hours getting ready and hours cleaning up afterward. Premixed paints, electric-drill attachments and self-dispensing calking guns make short

1657

work of preparation. Cleaning up is a soap-and-water job for the rubber paints, or a quick dip in special cleaners for the oils. Disposable drop-cloths and paper paint pails are used once and thrown away.

In this section are some tips on techniques and tools that make it easier to paint your house than ever before—not the way the "pro" does, perhaps, but with much the same results.

The term paint is used to include paints, varnishes, enamels, shellacs, lacquers, and stains.

• Paints are composed of mineral pigments, organic vehicles, and a variety of thinners all combined.

• Varnishes are resins dissolved in organic thinners.

• Enamels are pigmented varnishes.

• Shellac is lac gum dissolved in alcohol.

• Lacquers may be both pigmented or clear—the liquid portion usually is treated nitrocellulose dissolved in thinners.

• Stains may be pigmented oil or a penetrating type.

Many of these materials, such as paints, varnishes, and lacquers, are formulated for specific purposes:

• Outside house paints and exterior varnishes are intended to give good service when exposed to weathering.

• Interior wall paints are formulated to give excellent coverage and good washability.

• Floor enamels are made to withstand abrasion.

• Lacquers are formulated for rapid drying.

• There are also formulas which provide extra self-cleaning, fume-resisting, waterproofing, hardening, flexibility, mildew-resisting, resistance to fading, and breathing qualities.

Interior paints are used to obtain pleasing decorative effects, improve sanitary conditions, and insure better lighting. These paints may be divided into four types: wall primers; one-coat flats; flat, semigloss, and gloss; and water paints.

Wall primers or primer-sealers are intended to be applied directly to bare plaster, wallboard, and similar porous surfaces to provide a uniform, sealed surface for subsequent coats of paint. A typical wall primer may be made from varnish or bodied-oil vehicle and hiding pigments. It is intended to penetrate only slightly into porous surfaces. The primers are best applied with a wide wall brush.

One-coat flat paints are organic-solvent-thinned paints intended to accomplish priming, sealing, and finish coating in one operation. They are often sold in thin paste form so that additional inexpensive thinner may be added and mixed before application to increase the volume of paint by one-fourth or more.

Flat, semigloss, and gloss interior paints and enamels vary in degree of gloss, hiding power, and other properties. Paints giving the best hiding power are normally paints of lowest gloss, although some modern high-gloss enamels also have good hiding power.

Water-thinned interior paints are calcimine, casein, resin-emulsion, and gloss water paints. Calcimine consists of powdered whiting and clay mixed with an animal-glue binder and a preservative. It cannot be re-coated, but can be easily washed off

1658

before redecorating. (For more information, see section on *CALCIMINE*).

It is not necessary to remove casein before recoating but, if desired, it can be softened by washing with hot solutions of trisodium phosphate. Resin-emulsion paints, marketed in paste form, are to be thinned with water and, when properly made and applied, adhere well to plaster and provide a good decorative medium. They need not be removed before redecorating, provided the film is in sound condition. This is also true of gloss water paints.

New Paints Give You Pro's Skill

Painting your house will be easier than ever—if you get the right paint.

But it's going to be harder than ever to pick it.

Years ago, paint was paint. One kind looked, smelled, was applied and eventually dried much like another. Things are different now. Besides oil paints, you can choose from a new set of paints. It'll pay you to know about them.

• There are water paints you can use outside. (You clean your brushes under the faucet and use the garden hose to get spatters off the shrubbery.)

• There are finishes so tough they withstand even attacks from the neighbor's children.

Supergraphic zigzags of boldly painted earth tones establish a sense of kinetic energy in this basement family room.

1659

• There are paints that dry so fast you start the second coat as soon as you finish putting on the first.

• There are colors in glittering confusion.

No single product can do all these things. There are several types, all available under a variety of trade names. The trade names are, to put it kindly, confusing. For example, two brands of the new paints use "rubber" in their trade names, yet neither is a rubber-latex paint and each is actually an entirely different type of paint from the other. To get the right paint you have to read the fine print on the label and find out what is actually inside the can.

Vinyl is a cousin to the tough plastic used for upholstery and floor tiles, but it comes thinned with water ready for you to brush, roll or spray on. The label on the can may say vinyl, vinyl emulsion, polyvinyl acetate or PVA.

You can use vinyl on almost any

WHICH PAINT TO USE . . . AND WHERE — Exterior Surfaces

	House Paint	Water Repellant	Cement Base Paint	Rubber-Base Paint	Emulsion Paint	Penetrating Paint (Including Not Latex)	Aluminum Sealer	Wood Stain	Trim-and-Trellis Paint	Awning Paint	Spar Varnish	Porch-and-Deck Paint	Primer or Undercoater	Metal Primer
WOOD SIDING (Painted)	✔•												✔	
WOOD SIDING (Natural)					✔		✔			✔				
BRICK	✔•	✔	✔	✔	✔								✔	
CEMENT & CINDER BLOCK	✔•	✔	✔	✔	✔								✔	
ASBESTOS CEMENT	✔•			✔	✔								✔	
STUCCO	✔•	✔	✔	✔	✔								✔	
STONE	✔•	✔	✔	✔	✔								✔	
ASPHALT SHINGLE SIDING	✔•			✔			✔							
METAL SIDING	✔•								✔•					✔
WOOD FRAME WINDOWS	✔•								✔•				✔	
STEEL WINDOWS	✔•								✔•					✔
ALUMINUM WINDOWS	✔•								✔•					✔
SHUTTERS & OTHER TRIM									✔•			✔		
CLOTH AWNINGS										✔				
WOOD SHINGLE ROOF						✔								
WOOD PORCH FLOOR												✔		
CEMENT PORCH FLOOR			✔									✔		
COPPER SURFACES											✔			
GALVANIZED SURFACES	✔•						✔•	✔•		✔				✔
IRON SURFACES	✔•						✔•	✔•						✔

✔• Black dot indicates that a primer or sealer may be necessary before the finishing coat (unless surface has been previously finished.)

exterior except previously painted wood. It works fine on wood shingles and shakes, asbestos shingles, brick, stucco, concrete and masonry blocks. One manufacturer says you can even put it on wood clapboard if the clapboard is new and unprimed.

The major advantage of vinyl is the thinner—water. You get all the advantages of easy cleanup that have made interior water paints so popular.

Suppose it rains while you're working? Vinyl paint dries fast—as quickly as 10 to 30 minutes—and will withstand a shower after that time. It takes another 12 hours to "cure," by then forming an exceptionally tough, long-lasting film that stands up well against weather, sun, salt air and factory smoke.

One precaution: You can't paint with it in cold weather. The chemical reaction that transforms the water solution into a durable finish will not take place if the temperature is below 50°. (Conventional oil paints don't stick well in cold weather, either.)

Some manufacturers recommend their vinyl paints for interior as well as exterior use; others say no, not so good. There are vinyls made specifically for interiors.

Definitely good inside the house is a new vinyl primer-sealer to be used as a base coat under any paint. It dries in as little as 30 minutes. You can put it around a room and probably follow immediately with the finish coat. It can be applied with brush or roller.

Acrylic is the second new name for magic in paints. This is also a plastic-in-water. Solid acrylic you

Colors of the self-stick arrow on the window shade of this girl's bedroom are matched in the stripes painted down one wall and continued over a corner table.

know as the beautiful, glasslike Plexiglas and Lucite.

Inside the house is where acrylic shines. It dries faster than other types, and it keeps its color better, without yellowing. One disadvantage: It costs more.

Some acrylics are also recommended for exteriors (over the same kinds of materials as vinyl paints). Here it has a big advantage—you don't have to pick your painting weather so carefully. It can be applied on humid days and in cold sea-

1661

sons, so long as the temperature is a few degrees above freezing.

Alkyd is an old interior paint made newly popular by a change in solvent—a super-refined petroleum chemical that has almost no odor. It is not a water paint. You thin it and clean brushes with mineral spirits or turpentine, or, if you want to retain the odorless feature, with the new odorless solvent. (Ask the paint-store man for just that, odorless solvent.)

Alkyd has solid advantages overriding the slight cleanup inconvenience. It is exceptionally tough and very resistant to scrubbing. It stands up well in the trouble spots—trim, bathroom, kitchen. And it is easy to apply, producing a smooth, even finish free of streaks and brush marks.

The alkyds have little odor, but don't forget that the solvent is a petroleum product and its vapor is there even if you can't smell it. It can make you sick and it burns very easily, like the vapor of older paint solvents. So play safe: Keep windows open and keep flames away.

The old reliables are not to be overlooked either. Conventional *oil paints* can now be had in deodorized

1662

WHICH PAINT TO USE . . . AND WHERE   Interior Surfaces

Surface	FLAT PAINT	SEMI-GLOSS PAINT	ENAMEL	RUBBER BASE PAINT	EMULSION PAINT	CASEIN	INTERIOR VARNISH (INCLUDING LATEX)	SHELLAC	WAX (LIQUID OR PASTE)	WAX (EMULSION)	STAIN	WOOD SEALER	FLOOR VARNISH	FLOOR SEALER	CEMENT BASE PAINT OR ENAMEL	ALUMINUM PAINT	SEALER OR UNDERCOATER	METAL PRIMER
PLASTER WALLS & CEILING	✓•	✓•		✓	✓	✓											✓	
WALL BOARD	✓•	✓•		✓	✓	✓											✓	
WOOD PANELING	✓•	✓•		✓	✓•		✓	✓	✓		✓	✓					✓	
KITCHEN & BATHROOM WALLS		✓•	✓•	✓	✓												✓	
WOOD FLOORS							✓	✓	✓•	✓•	✓	✓•	✓•	✓•				
CONCRETE FLOORS									✓•	✓•	✓			✓				
VINYL & RUBBER TILE FLOORS									✓	✓								
ASPHALT TILE FLOORS										✓								
LINOLEUM							✓	✓	✓			✓	✓					
STAIR TREADS									✓		✓	✓	✓	✓				
STAIR RISERS	✓•	✓•	✓•	✓			✓	✓			✓	✓						
WOOD TRIM	✓•	✓•	✓•	✓	✓•		✓	✓	✓		✓						✓	
STEEL WINDOWS	✓•	✓•	✓•	✓												✓		✓
ALUMINUM WINDOWS	✓•	✓•	✓•	✓												✓		✓
WINDOW SILLS		✓•				✓												
STEEL CABINETS	✓•	✓•	✓•	✓														✓
HEATING DUCTS	✓•	✓•	✓•	✓												✓		✓
RADIATORS & HEATING PIPES	✓•	✓•	✓•	✓												✓		✓
OLD MASONRY	✓	✓	✓	✓	✓	✓									✓	✓	✓	
NEW MASONRY	✓•	✓•	✓•	✓	✓	•									✓		✓	

✓• Black dot indicates that a primer or sealer may be necessary before the finishing coat (unless surface has been previously finished.)

Exterior rollers now let you paint outside with the same ease as inside. Small doughnut-shaped roller (left) gets in corners, under edges of clapboards and between joints in vertical siding. Then large roller is used to fill in broad areas (right). Special long-nap roller also puts paint on brick, stucco and other rough-surface masonry. Paint tray clamps to side of ladder, can be adjusted to any angle.

version, made with the same odorless solvent used in the alkyds. And oil paint has much in its favor. It is sold everywhere; its virtues and faults are well established through centuries of use; it makes a tough film on almost any surface; it offers the greatest color range; and it is often cheaper.

Water-thinned *rubber-latex* paint is already an old reliable, though it is only about 20 years old. It accounts for a big percentage of all paint sold and is still the most widely available of the easy-to-use finishes. One new type is a combination vinyl-rubber paint that is said to do a better job on interiors than either vinyl or rubber alone because it dries faster, lasts longer and has less sheen.

Paint Selection

Most paints are purchased ready-mixed but, in their selection, consideration should be given to the fact that surfaces vary in their adaptability to paint and atmospheric or other conditions having an adverse effect on paint performance. In addition to the normal weathering action of sun and rain, outside house paints are sometimes exposed to other attacking elements, such as corrosive fumes from factories or excessive amounts of wind-driven dust.

For localities where such conditions exist, self-cleaning paints should be selected. These paints are usually so designated on the label. Concrete, plaster, and metal surfaces each present special problems in painting. For instance, paint for use on masonry or new plaster must be resistant to dampness and alkalies, and paints used on steel must have rust-inhibitive properties.

Color—The paint makers are out to sell the lady of the house and color is their come-on. They are tempting her with a kaleidoscope's variety; one firm offers more than 6,000 different shades.

1663

Here's the Score on the Newest Paints	Emulsion Finishes				Solvent Finishes	
	RUBBER	VINYL	RUBBER VINYL	ACRYLIC	ALKYD	OIL
Exterior	No*	Most	No	Some	No	Most
Interior	Yes	Some	Yes	Most	Yes	Some
Thin With	Water	Water (Unless can label specifies special reducer)	Water	Water	Mineral spirits, turpentine or odorless solvent if paint is odorless type	Mineral spirits, turpentine or odorless solvent if paint is odorless type
Clean Up With	Water	Water	Water	Water	Mineral spirits, turpentine or odorless solvent	Mineral spirits, turpentine or odorless solvent
Drying Time (Time between coats)	3–4 Hours	2 Hours	2 Hours	1–2 Hours	Overnight	Exterior: 2–3 Days Interior: 8 hours

*Generally not recommended for exterior use, but some special types are available for outdoor use.

Paper paint pails save buying and cleaning more expensive metal ones, are handy for mixing. Costing only a few cents, they're used once, then thrown away.

Practically every manufacturer has a "color system," a fat book of color chips with instructions for duplicating each chip. This is accomplished by intermixing cans of colored paint, by adding a concentrated color to a can of white or colored paint, or by adding concentrated color or colors to a can of neutral "base" paint. And for those who don't want any guesswork there's the Color Carousel that mixes the paints right in the store. Whatever the method, the result is a range of colors such as no amateur painter has seen.

Mixing

Paste paints, such as aluminum, resin-emulsion, and lead-in-oil, should be stirred with a stiff paddle and reduced to painting consistency with the liquids recommended on the manufacturer's labels.

Paints in powdered form require the addition of a liquid to prepare them for use. The manufacturer's directions as to the amount of oil, varnish, water, or other vehicle required should be followed.

"Boxing" is a good method of mixing paints. Since paint is a mixture of solids and liquids, it is important that it be mixed thoroughly before using. To do this, the greater portion of the liquid contents of the can should be poured in a clean bucket somewhat larger than the paint can. Then, with a stiff paddle, the settled pigment in the original container should be loosened and any lumps broken up. After this, mix the material in the container thoroughly, using a figure 8 motion, and follow with a lifting and beating motion. Continue stirring the mixture vigorously while slowly adding the liquid that was previously poured off the top. Complete the mixing by pouring the paint back and forth from one container to the other several times until the entire amount is of uniform consistency .

Paste and powder paints should be mixed in quantities sufficient for immediate use only, as these materials often become unfit for application if allowed to stand.

If paints have been allowed to stand and hard lumps or skin have formed, the skin or scum should be removed, after which the paint can be stirred and strained through screen wire or through one or two thicknesses of cheesecloth.

If a desired shade is not obtainable in custom- or ready-mixed paints, white paints may be tinted with colors-in-oil. To do this, mix the color-in-oil with a small amount of turpentine or mineral spirits and stir this into the white paint, a little at a time. If a blended color is desired, more than one color may be added, such as a chrome green and chrome yellow pigments to produce a lettuce green shade.

Painting—Basic Preparation of Surface

A satisfactory paint job requires cleaning, scraping, sanding, and puttying the surface prior to application of the paint. Do not try to cover chipped or cracked paint on woodwork. If dirt and rough spots are painted over, the new coating may peel, crack, blister, or wrinkle.

To prepare a surface for repainting, all loose paint should be removed with a putty knife or wire brush, rough spots sanded, and bare spots given a priming coat after the edges of the old paint film have been "feathered" or tapered off with sandpaper or steel wool. Nail holes should be filled with putty after the priming coat is applied and, where a surface has been patched, the new surface should be primed before succeeding coats are put on.

To remove paint from any surface, you have a choice of four different methods; you can use:

1. sandpaper, either by hand or with a powered sander

1665

2. heat, with a blowtorch or an electric paint remover

3. special scrapers designed to "plane" the layers of paint off the surfaces

4. a chemical paint remover.

Using Chemical Removers

There are many different chemical paint removers available. Some come in powdered form and have to be mixed, others come in pressurized aerosol cans and others come in liquid form, ready-mixed, under various trade names such as Wonder-Paste.

To use the liquid chemical removers, you need a full-haired brush, a 2″ scraping knife, a bucket for the remover, steel wool, drop-cloths, wire brush, cloths, alcohol for washing the surface after the paint has been scraped off.

The paint remover is applied with a brush, laying it on with the flat side of the brush, in one direction only (as shown in the accompanying photograph). Give it a good full coat for you should not go back and brush over it again. Continue to apply the remover over the remainder of the area, covering as much as you can in twenty minutes.

Once the twenty minutes are up, go back to where you started with a scraping knife. Test to see if the film has softened all the way down to the wood. If it has, go ahead and scrape off the paint layer. If the film has not softened all the way down to the wood, recoat the area again in the same manner as you did before.

Unless the finish is very old, two coats and one hour of time will be sufficient to soften the whole paint film. Don't rush the remover. Let it do all the hard work! If more time is needed, allow it! On extremely heavily coated surfaces, a third coat of the remover may be necessary.

Photographs courtesy of Wilson Imperial Co.

Chemical paint removers should be laid on with the flat side of the brush. Unlike paint, it should not be "worked out" or spread over the surface. Furthermore, do not go over an area once the remover has been applied, unless another coat is needed.

Once the chemical remover has loosened the paint film, use a putty knife or scraper to peel off the old paint layers down to the bare wood.

After you have scraped the paint from the surface, wash with cloths saturated with alcohol. When using removers, it generally will not be necessary to sand the surface since the remover does not raise the grain. However, check the grain by hand; if it's raised, then sand with fine sandpaper until smooth.

Using a Blowtorch

Extreme care is necessary when working with a blowtorch to remove paint to make certain that you do not violate safety rules concerning fire. Do not work near open windows and flying curtains; make certain that there is nothing inflammable about. When removing paint from around a window, keep the torch moving and avoid playing the flame on the glass—it's likely to crack it.

It is best to keep the torch in motion all the time you are playing the flame on the painted surface. If the paint starts to burn, you are holding the torch too close. Hold the blowtorch close enough to heat the paint film, but not to start a fire.

Furthermore, by continually moving the torch, you will avoid the possibility of scorching the wood. If you are removing paint from metal, make certain not to touch any part, even where the torch did not heat it. The metal conducts heat and the entire piece may cause a burn or even start a fire if you are not careful.

Also see *SOLDERING* and *TORCHES*.

Using Sanders and Scrapers

There are many different types of scrapers that can be used to remove paint. Some are flat surfaces while others are made irregular in order to

Blue painted walls of this living room complement tastefully the wallpaper of both the entrance foyer at left and the dining room at the rear.

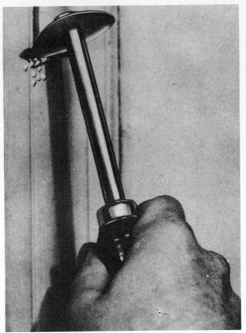

Photograph courtesy of Red Devil Tools.

Scrapers come in many shapes, depending upon the job for which they are designed to do. This "Ogee" or "Half-Ogee" hand scraper is made to remove old paint from crevices and recesses, which cannot be reached with flat scrapers or putty knives.

1667

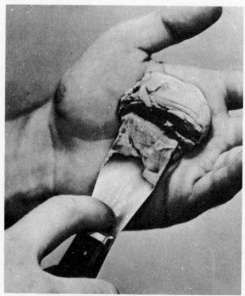

Sanding new wood surfaces smooth can be done effectively with a hand sanding block. Remember to sand with the grain finishing the job with #00 or finer paper. See **Abrasives**.

Photographs courtesy of Red Devil Tools.
Any holes or cracks in the wood surfaces should be filled with wood putty, forced into the openings with a putty knife.

1668

reach into grooves around moldings or trim.

Sanding requires care, especially when working with a powered sander.

In using the latter, keep the sander moving at all times so that you do not "eat" into the wood and cause an uneven surface.

Also see *ABRASIVES* and *SANDERS*.

New Interior Wood Surfaces

New interior wood surfaces generally can be cleaned simply by wiping with a rag soaked in solvent such as mineral spirits or turpentine. This will remove dust, greasy film and grimy dirt. If oil or wax has been spilled on the surface, remove by repeated solvent washings followed by immediate wipings with a clean, dry rag.

If the surface is to be varnished, shellacked, or finished in natural wood, sand to a smooth surface. Sand with the grain using #2 paper for rough and #00 or finer for finish sanding. Dust with a moist rag after sanding.

On open-grain woods such as oak, ash, hickory, mahogany and chestnut, apply one coat of clean or stained wood filler following manufacturer's directions. Close-grained woods such as maple, pine, cherry, or birch should be stained without filler. After the application of filler or stain and one coat of finish, putty-up nail holes and imperfections. Tint putty by mixing with small amount of stain and press into nail hole with thumb. Cut off with forward stroke of putty knife and smooth with a backstroke.

The reason that the filler or stain and one coat of finish are applied prior to puttying is to prevent the wood from absorbing the vehicle from the putty and becoming discolored. The absorption would also make the putty hard and brittle, eventually causing it to chip out.

If the surface is to be painted, sand as in the case of varnish, shellac or natural finish, wipe with moist cloth, apply one coat of wood primer, putty the imperfections, and follow with coat of enamel undercoat. Surface is then ready for any desired paint or enamel.

Painted Interior Wood Surfaces

Previously painted wood surfaces should be cleaned by wiping with a rag wet with a solvent such as mineral spirits or turpentine and immediately wiped dry with a clean rag. This should be done while the surface is wet, otherwise evaporation of the solvent will simply re-deposit the oils, grease, and dirt. If the surfaces are not waxed they may be cleaned with a solution of household kitchen detergent followed by thorough rinsing with clear water.

If the old paint or varnish is badly cracked, crazed, or wrinkled, it should be removed to the bare wood before repainting. This can be done with a chemical paint remover and 1½″ or 2½″ wood scraper.

Dirt should be cleaned from crevices and recesses using an "ogee" or "half ogee" scraper. If it is desired to remove moldings use a molding remover. It is good practice to scuff the surface of the old paint lightly with fine sandpaper, in the interests of better adhesion.

On restaining work, particularly if the color of stain is to be changed, it is necessary to remove all old finishes down to the bare wood.

Where a stain color change is involved, try bleaching with a commercial wood bleach to lighten the stain that has penetrated into the wood. The surface should then be refinished as outlined above for new wood.

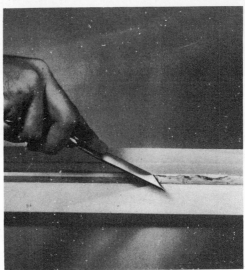

1669

Old paint can be removed from wood by applying a chemical paint remover or heating the surface with a blowtorch and then scraping the painted film off with a putty knife.

Sometimes it is necessary to remove old painted moldings. For example, if you wish to remove the paint and bleach the wood for a light natural finish. In such cases, use a molding chisel, shown here.

Plaster Walls

For new plaster walls, go over walls thoroughly to see that they are smooth, knocking off any mortar or plaster splotches with a 1¼″ putty knife. Remove all dust from walls with a vacuum cleaner. Allow walls to season for 3 to 6 months before painting, or paint them with an alkali-resistant finish as the first coat.

Painted plaster walls should be cleaned, and cracks and broken areas repaired before repainting.

Peeling paint should be removed with a wall scraper.

To patch larger-than-hairline cracks (hairline cracks can be covered with sealer), first form a keyway for new plaster. Do not shape crack into a "V" because patched plaster later may fall out. Wide deep cracks should be filled with oakum or similar material to within ⅛″ of the surface. Moisten crack before plastering. Spray water into the cracks, do not brush in. Brushing may sweep dirt into the base plaster and new plaster won't stick. Water can be sprayed into cracks by flicking from the end of a small brush. Apply plaster to cracks with a putty knife, the 1¼″ size being recommended. Paint patched cracks color of walls or ceiling to prevent showing through when repainted.

To repair small cracks and broken areas, apply spackling (also spelled "spachtling"), which is somewhat like patching plaster, with a 5″ spackling knife. For larger areas use patching plaster. Such patched areas should be sanded smooth the next day.

One coat of paint usually is sufficient although two sometimes are required. Two may be needed when going from a dark shade to a light shade or if the original paint is in very bad condition. Brush or roller may be used.

Preparation of Papered Walls for Painting

There are several ways to remove wallpaper, when required, before painting the wall (see later section on *PAINTING—INTERIOR*).

Many people still use plain water, which will work after a fashion, but it is a slow and laborsome job. The warm water is applied with a sponge, brush or cloth. After the surface has been soaking for about 10 to 15 minutes, use a scraper to peel the paper off. Start at the top, keeping the blade against the wall. If the scraper is lifted at each stroke, it may nick the plaster or plasterboard each time it is reapplied and these nicks will have to be patched.

Many wallpapers made and sold in recent years have been "washable." This means that they resist water and permit washing. Therefore, plain water is not very effective when removing this type of wallpaper.

Wallpaper steamers (available on a rental basis from many hardware stores) have been in use for many years. They will do a good job of loosening the paper from the wall surface, but in the process they will saturate the entire room. Furthermore, if you have drywall construction, the steamer may loosen the protective top coat of the wall surfacing material itself.

Chemical wallpaper removers have gained in popularity because they are easier to use. Many of them are sold in concentrated form and are diluted in warm water. The solu-

Removing old paint with a chemical paint remover is one way to insure a good painting job. This badly damaged exterior wood wall has had its paint removed with a chemical remover; once the paint film has softened, it's simple to remove it with a scraper or putty knife.

Removal of wallpaper is quick and easy with chemical wallpaper removers. Mix the concentrated solution with warm water and apply to the paper. Then scrape it loose without fear of damaging the surface of the wall proper.

Photographs courtesy of Wilson Imperial Co.

tion can be applied with a brush, sponge or even a paint roller. After the paper has been saturated, it will peel off quickly and easily.

Outdoor Wood

The first step in preparing new outdoor wood surfaces for painting is to seal all knots with shellac or with the newer vinyl resin-type knot sealers. Next, apply a prime coat of paint and then putty up all cracks and nail holes. Calk all joints and openings and proceed with final painting.

For painted outdoor wood surfaces, nail down all loose boards, preferably with aluminum nails. Countersink nails and fill nail holes with putty. Scrape off all loose or scaling paint. If old paint is peeling, checked or blistered, remove with tungsten carbide scraper; by burning with a torch and scraping with long handled putty knife or scraper; or by using a wax-free paint and varnish remover and scraper.

In repainting sash, scrape away loose putty, and prepaint the sash and that portion of the glass which will be covered by putty. Apply new putty when paint dries. Allow a few days for putty to harden.

Metal Surfaces

Remove peeling paint with carbide scraper and remove rust with emery cloth. Touch-up exposed areas with rust inhibitor, let dry and apply new paint. Allow new downspouts and gutters to stand a year before painting. They will oxidize

1671

and absorb paint better. If it is desired to paint immediately, age with strong vinegar or diluted acetic acid, wash clean and apply prime coat.

Masonry Walls

Peeling paint can be removed from smooth cement with a carbide scraper, or a wire brush may do the job on rough cement. If not, virtually nothing short of sand or steam blasting will do the job. Repaint when surface is clean and dry. (If there is a moisture or leakage problem, this must be corrected before painting.)

Painting—Brushes and Rollers

You have a choice of three different "tools" with which to paint.

• You can use the oldest and most common tool—the paint brush,

• or you can use the paint roller, which has advanced considerably in design since it was introduced about 1945,

• or there is the paint sprayer.

Which tool you use depends upon the job to be done and your skill. Here are some facts about each:

Brushes—Good quality brushes are not cheap, but a good brush, properly cared for, can last many years in the hands of a homeowner. Most handymen possess sufficient skill to use a brush but many do not know the fine techniques necessary for a professional-looking job. See section on *BRUSHES*.

Rollers—It is possible for the average homeowner to do a better paint job with a roller than with a brush. It is easy to develop the right

1672

skills and before you know it, you can work like a professional.

Sprayers—Considerable practice is needed in order to do a top-notch job with a sprayer. A poor sprayer in inexperienced hands will result in a poor job; so will a good sprayer in inexperienced hands. However, once you acquire the few simple skills, it is possible to do an outstanding job with a sprayer.

Covers for Rollers

The first practical paint-roller cover material, developed about 1945, was wool. However, after a great number of covers were used, it was found that wool did not provide a practical all-purpose cover. Sheep coming from different climates have different types of coats. The most desirable skin for a wool paint roller was a heavy, dense but medium-fine wool that was straight. Production methods were slow, because each skin had to be measured and only the select covers could be cut out. The remainder was scrapped. All of this was done with hand labor.

Wool covers are fine for oil flat paints. They are useless in the new water and rubber base paints. Because wool absorbs roughly 14%, it soaks to the core, and the fibrous, resilient, paint-holding structure of the wool is lost, thereby making it worthless.

As a result, new fabric coverings were developed.

Dynel has the all-purpose characteristics needed to make a fine paint roller. It absorbs less than ½% water; therefore, it is excellent for water base paints. In oil base paints it works as well as wool. Because it is man-made, the denier and density

The paintbrush defects shown at right, all result from misuse of the brush: Painting with side of brush is a major cause of "fingering." If you use a wide brush to paint pipes and similar surfaces it will take a fishtail shape. Swelling may occur if you dip the brush too deeply. If paint hardens in the heel, it will swell the ferrule. Avoid curling by hanging the brush up.

FINGERING

PAINTING POINTERS

1.

FISHTAILING

2.

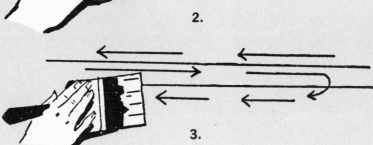

3.

In painting exterior surfaces, you can get a smoother and more uniform job by daubing paint on in spots (1) before stroking. Then use long, leveling brush strokes (2) to spread the paint smoothly. Finish the brush stroke (3) in a zigzag path and you'll have a good-looking job.

CURLING

SWELLING

Blend each stroke toward the wet paint area, not away from it, to avoid ridges and lap marks.

Keep bristles pointed downward, or at least tilted at an angle below the horizontal, while you work. Tilt a brush upward only for ceiling work. Pointing the bristles down helps keep paint from running into the heel. If the paint hardens in the heel it will swell the ferrule and perhaps ruin the brush. For the same reason, dip a brush no more than halfway into paint each time you charge it.

PAINTING POINTERS

Wrap brush for storage, using heavy paper, oilcloth or aluminum foil. Be sure that the bristles lie straight and that end of brush is not compressed by the wrapping. Suspend the brush with the bristles down. If it's a fine-quality brush used in oil paints, saturate the brush with linseed oil before wrapping it.

Brush storage rack can be made by driving short nails part way into ¾″ plywood so brushes can rest on handles. Mount board on door or shop wall. Wrap brushes before storage.

Sketches courtesy of Baker Brush Co.

Store brushes in solvent overnight, suspending them in the container by one of the methods illustrated. In method at far right, the handle is tied to thin stick extending beyond bristles. Brush can then stand upright without resting on bristles.

1674

of the cover are controlled to meet exact specifications.

Lonel is one of the finest of all synthetic paint roller fabrics on the market, and the most versatile. It is a fabric that will work in practically any kind of oil or water base paint, be it interior or exterior, gloss or flat.

The following paragraphs describe the specialized fabrics which have been developed to do specific jobs with special types of paint.

1. *Mohair*—Mohair rollers are short-nap rollers, less than ¼″ in depth. This is a woven material that is specially designed to do a good job of applying heavy bodied enamels without showing a stipple.

2. *Dacron*—Dacron is the latest find in a roller material that is exceedingly fine in denier. It is woven into a cover that is especially designed to apply heavy-bodied exterior paints without showing an undue amount of stipple.

3. *Carpet and Fleecy Types*—These covers are used exclusively to apply oil-base paints. The different textures of these two fabrics produce different kinds of finishes, from sand float to Spanish textures.

4. *Sponge Rubber*—The sponge rubber roller accomplishes the same thing as carpet and fleecy types, but works successfully with water base texture paints.

The roller industry is constantly striving to develop and produce new types of fabrics that will apply paints better and faster than anything known before. Fabrics that are in test and have been used are: long cotton staples, Orlon, nylon, Acrilan, acrylics, etc.

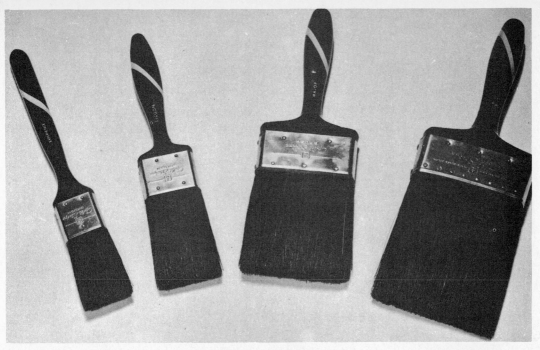

BRUSH NOTES

1. Select a quality brush for the job it is designed to do. Here (left to right) are: 1½" sash brush, 2" trim brush, 3½" and 4" wall brushes.

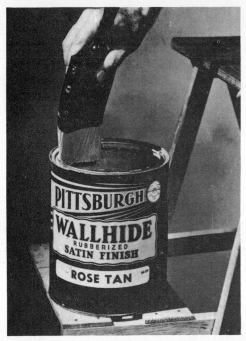

1675

2. When using a paint brush, dip it about half the length of the bristles into the can of paint. You should never get the ferrule (metal band) wet with paint.

3. Lightly wipe the excess paint off the brush by pressing it against the side of the can. Note that pressure is exerted just above the ends of the bristles.

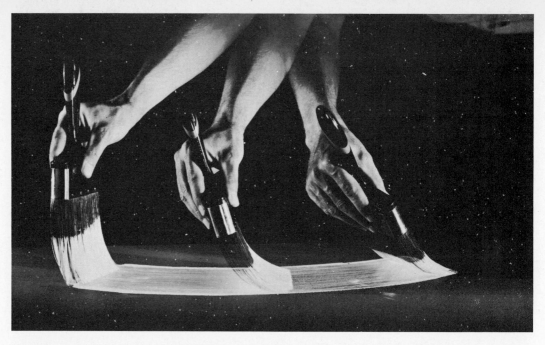

4. Lay the paint on with short, slightly curved strokes, lifting the brush gradually at the end of the stroke. Note the correct way to hold the brush.

1676

5. After you have finished painting, clean the brush thoroughly by submerging it and working the solvent well into the bristles. Use the right solvent for the paint.

6. Squeeze the bristles between the thumb and your fingers to work the paint out of the heel of the brush. It is essential not to leave any paint on the bristles.

Stock lumber, painted to match the furniture, outlines the papered wall, providing bright accent in this teen's room.

8. When storing a brush, one that will be used again shortly, do not set it on its bristles! Instead, suspend it in a container or jar with solvent up to the ferrule.

1677

7. After all the paint has been removed and the solvent squeezed out of the bristles, comb the brush. This will reset the bristles and keep them working.

Types of Rollers

Dip Roller—The most popular rollers developed are of the dip type. They range in size from 1″ to 13½″.

They work for such highly specialized uses as painting the underside of clapboard with the beveled 1″ roller (to be finished off with a 5½″ roller).

Corner rollers that are used to trace around ceilings, corners, and moldings prepare the way for 7″ or 9″ rollers which are used to finish the large surface of the wall.

There are 9″ to 13½″ rollers that are used for industrial purposes to cover large areas rapidly with the use of extension handles.

Floor to ceiling may be reached with 48″ handles, and greater distances may be reached with an aluminum, telescopic extension handle.

Short and long nap rollers made of the previously discussed fabrics are designed to paint almost any type of surface, including smooth clapboard walls on the exterior of a house, shingles and stucco or masonry blocks.

Interior rollers can paint any type of wall construction. A roller applies the paint in an even paint film, applying only the proper amount of paint. Too little or too much paint cannot be applied with the roller, which works very much like a roller on a printing press. If a surplus of paint is applied to the wall, the roller will pick up the excess and apply it to a dry surface. When exactly the right amount of paint has been applied to a surface, the roller cannot

1678

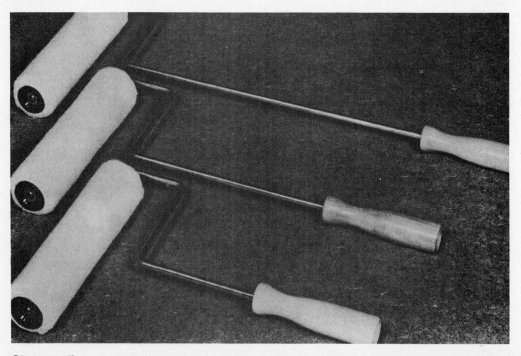

Dip-type rollers are made in a variety of sizes with different types of coverings designed for special surfaces. Here are three rollers, 14″, 18″ and 24″ long; the length of the handle varies in order to enable you to reach out-of-the-way places.

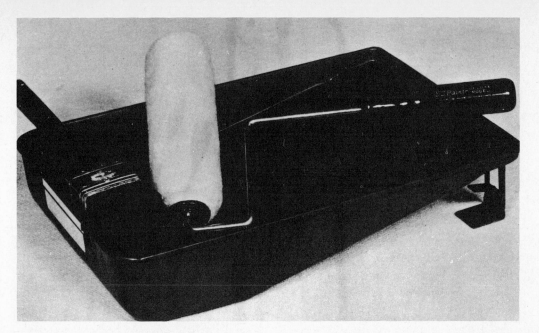

Photographs courtesy of E Z Paintr Corp.

pick this up and spread it out too thinly. In other words, a roller can apply just so much paint and no more. The amount put on is the correct amount.

Fountain Model Rollers—These are very practical to apply either flats or enamels to a wall. The advantage of a fountain model roller is that it eliminates dipping. Up to a pint of paint can be poured into a fountain roller, which is the reservoir for the excess paint. The cover is constructed to permit the paint to ooze through the fabric and be rolled onto the surface.

The first fountain rollers developed were constructed of metal, which made them heavy. Modern fountain rollers are constructed with nylon parts that are long-wearing, strong, and light. The inside fabric, which acts as the resilient part of the roller, is lonel, woven into a cushion, and is covered with a sleeve of nylon which creates a thin, even, smooth surface with any kind of paint.

Dip-type rollers come with paint trays. This tray is used for interior painting and conveniently fits onto any step ladder. A special rest is available in order to hold a brush on the tray.

Fountain type rollers are often used by home handymen. Instead of dipping the roller into the tray to pick up the paint, the paint is poured into the cylinder.

Pressure Rollers—These are designed wholly for professional use. Such rollers are ideally used in large buildings such as schools, hospitals, warehouses, etc., where there are large surfaces, hallways, or rooms in which a single color is used. A pressure roller consists of a three-gallon material tank, from which an air-pressure pump ejects paint through a 15′ hose and into the base of a 7″ paint roller. The amount of paint that is allowed to flow into the roller

1679

is adjusted by a button in the handle. A pressure roller paints in a fraction of the time required by conventional methods, since it is basically designed for regulated, constant use.

Roller Cores

Construction of the various roller cover fabrics and their uses have already been discussed. However, there are three basic constructions of cores about which the covers are constructed:

1. *Wire* is superior to all other cores because of its plated, rustproof characteristics. It can be reused many times and formed into a perfect round shape when it is placed over the roller's adjustable drum. Wire is not affected by heat, cold, water, or oil.

2. *Plastic* cores constitute the middle quality of roller core construction. Plastic is practical. Because of its smooth inside diameter, it slips on and off roller handles quickly and easily. It is solvent-proof and durable.

3. *Fiber* cores are impregnated with waterproof and oilproof compounds to make them stand up in either water or oil base paints. They are lower in price than those of the two other cores. Because of its cheapness, fiber may be used once in a given color, then disposed of, rather than having to clean it for reuse. Fiber is serviceable and durable.

Roller Technique

As more and more Americans join the ranks of home decorators, the paint roller has become an important part of everyday life. Rollers now make it possible to paint expertly, with greater ease and with almost no mess. As with any job, a few rules of advance know-how can greatly lighten the task.

There is scarcely anything which the roller cannot paint easily and swiftly. Paint may be rolled right over wallpaper, plaster, wallboard,

For exterior use, a specially designed tray is used. It comes with a handy swivel hook which grips onto an outside ladder. Note the two different rollers; one is a "doughnut" shape used to paint inside of corners or edges of clapboard trim. The other is a 5½" dip-type roller for narrow surfaces, such as the face of clapboards.

1680

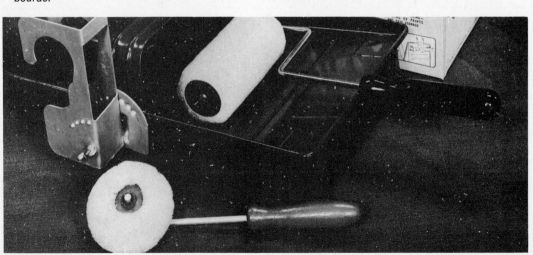

You can paint your own patterns on the wall with a design roller. There are many different patterns available from which to choose. It works like an ordinary dip-type roller; the roller is soaked in paint and transfers the paint to the design roller, which in turn transfers the paint to the wall.

Wire fences are easy to paint in almost a single stroke. Extra long-nap rollers are used and, as they are rolled across the face of the wire fence, the paint is applied to the front and sides of the wires.

Photographs courtesy of E Z Paintr Corp.

More like a miniature blackboard eraser, this "roller" is designed for painting window sash trim. It's almost impossible to get paint on the glass.

If you have large surfaces to be painted, such as a patio floor or a basement floor, special rollers with handles are available for the job. The long nap of the rollers gets the paint into all the crevices.

1681

brick, clapboard, concrete, and other surfaces. Even wire fences can be painted by a long-nap roller.

Oil, rubber base, and water base paints can be used with equal success with rollers. These include flats, gloss and semi-gloss, enamels, sizing, varnish, aluminum paint, and shellac. Most of these can be used just as they come from the can. Ordinary instructions should be followed if thinning is needed.

The surface to be painted should be prepared as for any brush or spray painting; clean and free from oil, dust, or foreign matter. If the surface is new, a primer coat may be essential, but follow instructions on the label of the finishing material to be used.

To begin painting, the roller tray, which can be placed conveniently on the floor or table, or attached to the ladder top or rung, should be filled to the "shore line," about half way up its slanted surface. Lining the tray with heavy paper or foil will save cleaning and permit quick changes of color.

Before actually painting the main surface area, a trim roller, a brush or one of several special devices which will be mentioned should be used progressively along the edges of the ceiling, floor, and woodwork. Do not trim the edges of more than one wall at a time, however. This will prevent shading.

The large roller should be loaded by rolling into the "shore line" of the paint, then back and forth on the ribbed surface of the tray to remove excess. Paint is applied to the surface with an easy back and forth rolling motion in any direction. Some "pros" recommend a criss-cross starting

1682

stroke. Be sure to keep the roller on the wall without spinning at the end of the stroke, and progress slowly and carefully into the previously trimmed edge, to within 1½″ of windows, corners and edges.

"Roller" Aids

There are several devices which provide the home decorator with invaluable supplementary tools to meet the problems of painting in corners and other hard-to-get-at areas. One of these is a 3″x5″ wool surface padding which gives a finish of roller rather than brush consistency. A protective blade permits it to be used against ceiling, moldings, etc., without smearing. An extension handle facilitates painting behind radiators, pipes, and similar awkward spots.

Another device is a small felt surface mounted on a plastic handle. This can be drawn over window sash and other edges without allowing paint to run over. A guard blade prevents smearing. With such helpful gadgets as these, the need for masking tape is eliminated.

Painting ceilings, one of the messiest painting problems, is effortless with the long-handle roller. For greater than usual heights, there has recently been introduced a lightweight aluminum telescopic extension handle, to which a regular roller may be attached for reaching up to 14′.

There are three important tips for success in ceiling painting:

1. The roller should be worked easily back and forth across the narrowest dimension.

2. Care should be taken not to lift the roller from the surface nor to spin it.

3. Work should not be stopped until the entire ceiling is completed (this will prevent lapping).

There is no more bending, stooping, or tedious kneeling to floor painting with a long-handled roller or regular roller attached to an extension handle. Floors of concrete, wood, or linoleum can be covered with equal success.

Exterior Rollers

The exterior roller is versatile. Barns, silos, storage tanks, wagons, pens, picket fences, brick walls, boats, garden furniture, porches, and children's playthings are only some of the myriad things on which the exterior roller set can do a first-rate job.

Exterior paint rollers are similar to interior rollers, and may be cared for in the same way. Exterior rollers are generally larger, and the fabric is of a different type, to prevent the heavier bodied paints from stippling.

Here are a few precautions which, together with directions ordinarily found on paint cans, will produce really professional results in exterior painting.

New, unpainted wood surfaces should be allowed to dry thoroughly before painting. Knots and resin streaks should be sealed with a modern knot sealer or shellac to prevent bleeding or discoloration of paint film. Before painting old surfaces, loose paint should be removed with a scraper. Necessary repairs should be made: loose boards nailed down; projecting nail heads secured; cracks and nailhead pits filled in with putty. Finally, the area should be sanded smooth.

When preparing concrete surfaces it is important to remember that no paint will adhere to a loose, crumbly surface, so all loose particles, dirt, etc., should be removed before painting. It is necessary to be sure that loose joints are routed out and "tuck pointed"; that cracks and crevices are filled; and that broken corners are replaced.

On clapboard walls the underedges should first be painted, one section at a time, with the small lap roller. Start at the top and work down. Follow with a 5½" roller on flat surfaces. Be sure that the roller contains no excess paint, and roll easily on the surface without spinning the end of the stroke.

If the surface of cement block or stucco is extremely rough, a long-nap roller is required. The long-nap roller is also effective on siding and shingles with deep crevices, as well as in such special work as painting wire fences.

Modern exterior roller trays have the gradually slanted surface of ordinary trays, but with a protective covering over the deeper end. Exterior trays may be attached to the sides of extension ladders, and fixed so that moving the ladder will not spill out of the tray. Still attached to the ladder, the tray may be moved to a vertical position and used as a pail for mixing paint. Another ladder lock permits the tray to be fastened to the top surface of a step ladder. This same ladder lock can be transposed into a carrying handle for the full tray when it is once again in vertical position.

Cleaning rollers has ceased to be a difficult problem. After the use of oil paint, the excess should first be squeezed out of the removable roller

1683

HANDLING A ROLLER

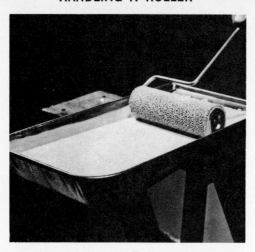

1. When using a roller, revolve it several times in the paint at the deep end of the tray. Then, get the surplus paint off the roller by squeezing it against the ramp of the tray.

cover. This may be done without messiness by using a handy squeegee especially made for this purpose. Another tip: place the cover inside of a plastic or heavy paper bag and squeeze by hand.

Next, the roller cover should be saturated with a specially prepared roller cleaner, or turpentine, fuel oil, kerosene, or mineral spirits. The cover should be agitated in the solution, squeezed dry, then the process repeated. After painting with latex or water paint, the cover is similarly cleansed, but with soap in lukewarm water followed by a very thorough rinsing.

Before storing, remember to wipe the roller dry. Storing in a plastic container keeps covers fresh and clean for an indefinite period of time.

2. Start the roller off with several criss-cross strokes on the area to be painted, then continue to work up and down to spread out the paint over the area.

3. After you have finished painting with a roller, clean it in the proper solvent. Agitate, squeeze out excess liquid and wipe the roller with a cloth. Then set cover aside to dry.

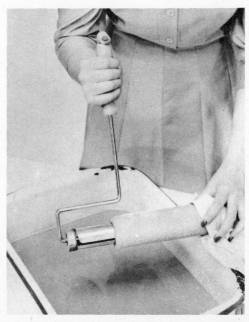

Painting—Common Failures

While it's true that no paint lasts forever, you have probably had some paints "fail" you. Within a matter of weeks or months, or even a year, there are imperfections, blisters; layers are peeling off. The term generally applied in such cases is "paint failure."

However, the chances are that it's not the paint's fault. Unless you have used an inferior paint, the cause of failure is either in your failure to prepare the surface properly to receive the paint or in your failure to apply the paint properly.

Of course, anyone who has wielded a paint brush immediately considers himself an experienced painter. Why, there's nothing to it—just put the paint on the brush and lay it on the surface. But painting is not that simple.

In the following parts of this section, there are detailed instructions on how to apply paint. For the present, however, let us concern ourselves with the "paint failures" and what we can do about them. Understanding why the paint failed is half the battle.

In the accompanying photographs, you will see some of the common types of paint failure. There is also

Checking is a minor paint failure; unless it is extensive, it can be ignored. It may be due to poor workmanship or the use of improperly formulated materials; maybe the undercoat was not dry when the final coat was applied. You can prevent checking by allowing sufficient drying time between coats. While some manufacturers say 24 hours are enough, it's better to wait 3 to 7 days between coats.

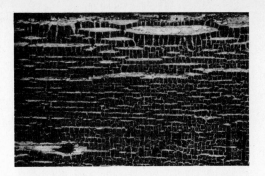

Alligatoring is an advanced form of checking, causing the paint film to take on the appearance of alligator skin, hence the name. It is usually caused by an improperly built-up paint film. Possibly, incompatible paints were used; perhaps the undercoat was not given sufficient time to dry; maybe the surface was never cleaned and the paint was applied over grease.

Blistering is a defect frequently caused by the construction of the house and not by the paint. It may be due to excessive moisture present behind the paint film. Maybe the wood was not dry when painted; maybe water seeped in behind the wood after it was painted and there is no way out but through the surface.

1685

Photographs courtesy of PPG Industries

Spotting is caused by unequal oil absorption. A poor paint will soon show its weakness by extensive spotting. Adequate sealing of the surface is the secret of a good paint job. There is no economy in insisting on a low price paint or doing a shoddy job.

Wrinkling is a leather-like surface on a paint film. It can be caused by too heavy a coat of paint, improper brushing or it may be due to an improper combination of oil and pigment in the finish coat.

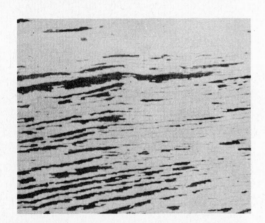

Cracking is sometimes caused by improperly made paints which dry too hard for the conditions of the particular job. The use of undercoats and finish coats of equal elasticity, possessing equal ability to expand and contract, will safeguard against this condition. Therefore, use the undercoat recommended by the manufacturer or one identical to it.

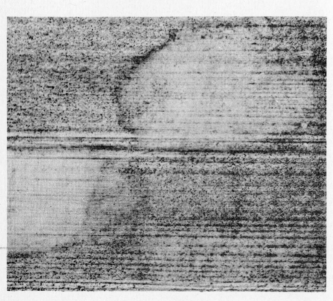

Staining is used to cover a variety of blemishes for which there are many causes. Water drips from metal (copper or iron pipe and gutters) can cause unsightly streaks. You can prevent this by painting the metal gutters and downspouts. Storm spots come from exposure to continuous rains and electrical storms. Usually weathering takes care of this damage and soon restores the original color to the paint film. When damp wood is painted, the water finds its way into the paint film carrying with it substances that cause brown stains. You can prevent this type of stain by making certain that the wood is seasoned and dry before painting. Structural defects must be watched for and eliminated; seal all knots to prevent the resin from seeping through and staining the paint film.

information about possible causes together with information about cures.

Paint Failure and Wood Rot

Sometimes paint failures are due to the improper preparation of the wood itself. Where wood is exposed to excessive moisture, more than paint is needed to keep it sound. It is best to treat the wood surfaces chemically to prevent wood rot and then paint over the treated wood.

Painting—Exterior Surfaces

For exterior wood and metal surfaces, painting should be done only in clear, dry weather and generally the temperature should not be below 50° F. When the weather is cold, work should be stopped early enough in the afternoon to allow the paint to set before a sudden drop in temperature occurs. Woodwork should be thoroughly dry and seasoned before paint is applied. Temperature conditions should be the same for painting exterior masonry as for wood and metal. Masonry surfaces must be dry if oil base paints are to be used, while other masonry paints such as cement-water and resin-emulsion may be applied to damp surfaces.

Sufficient time should be allowed between coats so that the paint film will dry hard before more paint is applied. Oil paints on exterior wood should dry at least 24 hours, several days' drying time being preferable.

Two-Coat Paint System

A minimum of three coats was formerly the accepted practice for initial painting on exterior wood, and this practice is still largely followed. However, by using special primers, two-coat paint systems for wood have been developed that are durable and satisfactory. The principle of the two-coat paint system is that as much paint is applied in two coats as normally would be applied in the three-coat method of painting. On smoothly planed wood, the usual spreading rate for three-coat painting is about 550 to 600 sq. ft. per gallon for the first or priming-coat paint and about 600 to 650 sq. ft. per gallon for each of the next two coats. In the two-coat paint system, the primer is spread at the rate of about 450 sq. ft. per gallon and the finish coat about 550 sq. ft. per gallon. Rough surfaces and weather-beaten wood require much more

Photograph courtesy of Valspar Corp.

Make certain that you cover all edges and spaces between boards when painting exterior wood.

1687

USE THE RIGHT PAINT

SHINGLES
Shingle stain

BODY
House paint

METAL SURFACES
Metal primer
House paint
Exterior enamel

TRIM
House paint
Trim-and-trellis paint

WINDOWS
Caulking compound
Putty

SCREENS
Screen enamel

PORCH FLOOR
Porch-and-deck paint

MASONRY
House paint
Cement base water paint
Transparent coating
Rubber base paint
Bituminous coating
for foundation

LAWN FURNITURE
Exterior enamel
Farm implement paint

Sketch courtesy of National Paint, Varnish and Lacquer Association

1688

paint than is indicated for smoothly planed wood.

Three-Coat Paint System

Mixed-pigment prepared paints are available for three-coat work, in addition to linseed-oil, white-lead paints which may be mixed on the job or purchased ready-mixed. The manufacturer's directions should be followed in thinning the first and second coats. It is sometimes advisable in moist atmospheres, particu-larly at the seashore, to add a small amount (1 pint to a gallon) of good exterior varnish to the top coat of paint. The varnish should first be tried in a small amount of paint to make sure that the two are compatible and that the varnish will not cause the paint to thicken.

Shingle Stains

Shingle stains are pigmented oil stains, similar to very fluid paints, which can be applied by dipping,

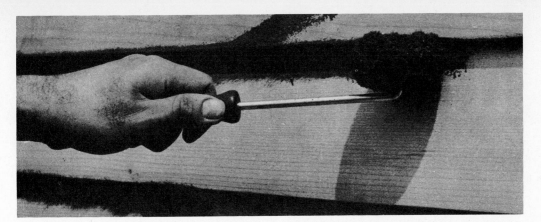

brushing, or spraying. They are intended for application to comparatively rough exterior wood surfaces where it is not necessary to bring out the grain and texture of the wood to which they are applied, and they dry to a matte or semi-transparent finish. Durable pigments, such as iron oxides, are used for the colors red through brown; chromium oxide, for green; and zinc oxide or white lead tinted with lampblack, for gray.

Shingle stains should not cake or change color in the container and when stirred should settle very slowly. With the exception of some dark brown stains, which are simply refined coal-tar creosote with volatile thinners, shingle stains are usually made from very finely ground pigments, drying oils, and volatile thinners. Many commercial shingle stains contain some creosote oil from coal tar or water-gas tar which is intended to act as a wood preservative. While pressure treatment with creosote is one of the most effective methods of preventing wood from rotting, the small amount that penetrates the wood from a single dip or brush treatment probably has very little effect.

Paint applied over creosote stain

The wider sections of the board are then given the finishing touches with a special 5½" roller. In this way, all surfaces and edges are protected with paint.

Photographs courtesy of E Z Paintr Corp.

1689

is likely to be ruined by the creosote bleeding through. If there is any possibility that the shingles may be painted at some future time, pigment oil shingle stains without creosote should be used.

Masonry Surfaces

Paints for masonry wall surfaces may be divided into four types: Cement water paint, resin-emulsion paint, oil paint, and paint containing rubber in the vehicle. These paints are also suitable for use on such masonry surfaces as foundations, gate posts, and fence or enclosure walls, but they should not be used on floors which are subject to abrasion. For such surfaces, a very hard-drying paint with good water resistance and gloss retention is recommended.

Cement-water paints are water-dilutable paints in which Portland cement is the binder. They are particularly suitable for application on damp, new, or open-textured masonry surfaces. These surfaces include those walls that are damp at the time of painting, or that may become damp after painting as a result of structural defects or other causes; new structures (less than 6 months old) which normally contain water-soluble alkaline salts; and open-textured surfaces such as cinder, concrete, and lightweight aggregate block. These paints are not recommended for stopping leakage through porous walls that are exposed to water pressure, particularly if the paint is applied to the inside of the wall. For such conditions, a coating of hot bituminous material applied to the outside of the wall is preferable.

Close-textured surfaces which are relatively dry, such as cast concrete, asbestos-cement siding, and tile, may be painted with resin-emulsion paint or paints containing rubber in the vehicle. Walls which are dry at the time of painting, and are so constructed as to remain dry after painting, may

Paint rollers can be used to cover brick. It is best to use a long nap roller so that the paint covers the brick surfaces and the mortar joints as well.

be decorated satisfactorily with oil paints.

CEMENT-WATER PAINT

Cement-water paints are water-dilutable paints, packaged in powder form. They are composed chiefly of Portland cement or Portland cement and lime and possess good decorating qualities or hiding power and color. However, when wetted, as by rain, they become somewhat translucent and darker in color. When again dry, the film returns to its original opaqueness and color.

To clean a surface for the application of cement-water paint, thoroughly remove all dust, dirt, and efflorescence, old coatings of whitewash, and flaking or scaling cement-water paint by brushing vigorously with a wire brush. Firmly adhering

1690

coatings of cement-water paint or cement-water paints which are "chalking" or "dusting" need not be removed, but should be brushed with a stiff bristle brush to make the surface uniform.

Before applying the paint, whether initially or on a previously painted surface, the masonry should be thoroughly wetted, preferably with a garden hose adjusted to produce a fine spray. A superficial dampening with a brush dipped in water is not adequate for exterior walls but may be satisfactory for cool basement walls. Usually, wetting the walls in one operation not more than an hour before painting is sufficient. The water should be applied so that each part is sprayed three or four times for about 10 seconds each, time being allowed between applications for the water to soak into the surface. If the surface dries rapidly, as it may in hot weather, it should be redampened slightly just before painting. The wall surface should be moist, not dripping wet when paint is applied.

Cement-water paint powder should be mixed with water in accordance with the manufacturer's directions. Paints may be tinted by adding suitable amounts of coloring pigments but, due to the difficulty of producing uniform colors by hand mixing, it is suggested that commercial brands of tinted paints be purchased which have been mill ground in the factory.

Cement-water paint should be applied in two coats. Preferably not less than 24 hours' drying time should be allowed between coats. The first coat should be slightly moistened with water before applying the second.

Most Portland cement paints cannot be satisfactorily applied with the ordinary hair-bristle paint brush. Proper application requires a brush with relatively short, stiff, fiber bristles such as fender brushes, ordinary scrub brushes, or roofers' brushes.

While thick films are to be avoided, there is a tendency to use too much water in cement-water paint and to brush it out too thin. Coatings applied in this manner may look well at first but will generally lose their opacity and protective value much sooner than thicker films. The proper spreading rate is difficult to estimate for Portland cement paint because of the difference in the texture of the masonry to be covered. However, on smooth masonry, 1 gallon of mixed paint should be sufficient to cover 100 sq. ft. with two coats; and, for rough masonry, 1 gallon should be sufficient to apply two coats to 50 sq. ft. of surface.

After painting it is desirable to sprinkle the freshly painted surface two or three times a day with a fog spray, such as is used for dampening walls prior to painting, and it is recommended that this be done between coats and for 2 days after the final coat, starting as soon as the paint has set, usually 6 to 12 hours after application.

RESIN-EMULSION PAINT

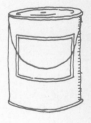

Resin-emulsion paints are water-thinned materials whose dry-film properties closely resemble those of a flat oil paint. They may be used on most porous masonry surfaces, including asbestos-cement siding, which has not been previously coated with a waterproofing compound. They should not be used on magnesite stucco.

To prepare the surface for resin-

1691

emulsion paints, remove by brushing or washing all dust, dirt, efflorescence, and loose particles from the surface; and also remove any flaking or scaling paint by scraping or wire brushing. Glossy areas should be dulled by sanding; oil, grease, and wax should be removed by scrubbing with mineral spirits. Then wash with water containing trisodium phosphate (about 2 ounces to the gallon), and rinse thoroughly with clean water.

Resin-emulsion paints are packaged in paste form and need to be thinned with water before being applied. They should be mixed in clean metal containers (not wood) in accordance with the directions given on the manufacturer's label and not allowed to stand after mixing for more than a week.

Resin-emulsion paint should be applied in two coats and the air temperature when painting should be above 50° F. A sizing or priming coat is not generally required except on open-textured masonry. For that, a cement-water paint containing sand should be used to fill the voids in the wall surface. On very warm days, it may be advisable to moisten the surface to be painted with water, prior to applying the paint. Resin-emulsion paint will dry in 1 to 4 hours, and may be recoated in 6 to 8 hours; the film becomes hard overnight. One gallon of the

1692

paste paint will cover approximately 200 to 450 sq. ft., depending upon the surface and the application. Brushes and spray guns should be washed with warm soapy water immediately after using.

Oil Paints

Oil paints intended for use on masonry are usually ready-mixed paints containing weather-resistant opaque pigments suspended in drying oils, resins, and thinners. They should be formulated so that the first coat seals the surface sufficiently to prevent spots or flashes of the second coat. Two coats are necessary for good hiding and durability.

Moisture back of the paint film will seriously impair the life of a coating of oil-base paint, therefore the application of oil paint to new masonry should be deferred until the walls have had time to dry. This may require 3 months to a year, de-

It's easy to paint rough concrete with a roller. This is a job that would take a long time and ruin a paint brush. But with a roller, you can apply the paint just as easily as if you were painting a flat interior wall.

Photograph courtesy of E Z Paintr Corp.

pending upon the thickness and porosity of the wall and the weather conditions. Because of the importance of preventing water from entering the walls after painting, repairs of structural defects, such as leaks around flashing, doors, and windows, should be made before applying oil-base paint.

Dust and dirt should be washed off and efflorescence should be brushed off with a stiff fiber or wire brush. All traces of oil should be removed with steel brushes, abrasive stones, or a lye solution. However, if the surface is badly stained, it should be lightly sandblasted.

Caution:—When using lye (caustic soda, sodium hydroxide), avoid splashing the eyes, skin, and clothing because it may cause burns.

Old coatings of organic paint or cement-base water paint in sound condition need not be removed. Whitewash or peeling, scaling, or flaking paints should be completely removed.

Oil paints should not be applied during damp or humid weather or when the temperature is below 50° F. At least 1 week of clear dry weather should precede the application of the first coat. As masonry surfaces tend to chill and collect condensed moisture, painting early in the morning and late afternoon should be avoided except in dry climates.

A minimum of 90 days' drying time should elapse before applying oil paint over a cement-water base or over mortar-filled joints and cracks. When it is not practicable to wait this long before painting, a calking compound rather than cement mortar should be used as a crack filler.

RUBBER-BASE PAINTS

There are two types of rubber-base paints, the rubber-solution and rubber-emulsion types.

Rubber-solution paints are available at most paint stores and usually sell for slightly more than oil-base masonry paints. They may be applied by brush, spray or roller to dry or slightly damp walls. They are suitable for painting asbestos-cement siding and shingles. These paints are also useful for "sealing in" stains on old masonry, and as protective primers under finishing coats of resin-emulsion or oil-base paints.

The same procedure outlined for preparing the surface for oil-base paints should be followed for rubber-base paints in removing dust, dirt, loose mortar, form oil, and efflorescence on dense surfaces.

Oil paint coatings must be removed before applying rubber-solution paints because the thinners used in these paints act as solvents for the oil paints. This is not necessary when applying rubber-emulsion paints over oil paints that are in good condition since they do not contain solvents that will soften the oil paints.

Rubber-base paints may be applied to dry or damp walls. It is usually necessary to thin the paint for the first coat, using the thinner recommended by the manufacturer, as some paint thinners are incompatible with rubber-base paints. The paint dries to the touch within three hours but, at least 18 hours' drying time should be allowed between coats, otherwise the succeeding coat will "lift" or soften the undercoat.

The brushing technique for rubber-base paints is the same as for applying enamels. "Back-brushing" or

1693

"working" the paint will cause it to roll and pull under the brush. As the paint tends to "set" rather quickly, it is advisable to work in shade rather than sunlight.

Brushes and spray guns should be cleaned with paint thinner immediately after they are used, because dry paint is difficult to redissolve once it has hardened.

Iron and Steel Surfaces

The chief reason for applying paint to exterior metalwork, particularly iron and steel, is to control and prevent corrosion. For best results two coats of priming paint followed by two coats of top or finishing paint are recommended on new work. For repainting, a spot coat followed by a full priming coat, and then one or two finish coats are rec-

To paint clapboards, first run your brush along the edge where one strip of siding overlaps the next. Then "spot-paint" a strip of the siding by striking your newly-filled brush to the wood at intervals. Join the spots with smooth brush action that spreads the paint evenly, making sure that you cover the entire board.

ommended. The usual recommended spreading rate of each coat of paint is about 600 sq. ft. per gallon. It should be stressed that the preparation of the surface, particularly steel, prior to painting is important, for unless the surface is properly cleaned so that the priming paint comes in direct contact with the metal, early failure of the paint film will probably occur.

Cleaning is the most important step in preparing metalwork for painting. It can be divided into two phases; the removal of oil and grease, and the removal of rust, dirt, scale, old paint, and moisture. All oil and grease should be removed before using mechanical methods of cleaning. The usual method is to wipe the surface with clean cloths and mineral spirits or carbon tetrachloride. The liquid as well as the cloths should be kept clean by frequent renewals to avoid leaving a thin, greasy film on the surface. When the oil and grease have been disposed of rust, scale, and old paint may be cleaned from the surface with wire brushes, steel wool, or motor-driven rotary brushes.

The paint should be applied in bright, warm weather to metal surfaces which are clean and dry. Painting should not be done early in the morning when the surface to be painted is damp from dew. Ample time should be allowed for each coat of paint to dry before applying the next coat.

Since the main function of a priming coat is to protect metal from corrosion, it should contain rust-inhibitive pigments. It can be applied by either brush or spray but particular care should be taken to cover the surface completely with the proper thick-

It just isn't possible, nor is it safe, to try to hold a paint tray in one hand and paint with the other when standing on a ladder. However, special trays are made for outdoor use; they attach conveniently and easily on the ladder.

ness of paint. Two coats of primer are recommended for new work. The second coat may be tinted to a slightly different color to make sure of adequate surface coverage. Ample time should be allowed for drying before application of succeeding coats.

Two practical coatings for steel surfaces are red-lead and iron oxide paints, red lead being used as a primer and iron oxide as a finishing material. Dull red and brown iron-oxide paints are economical for painting terne-plate roofs and structural metal. They are durable and are frequently referred to as roof and barn paint.

Red lead is available in three types: Type I, red-lead linseed oil paint which should be allowed to dry for a week between coats; type II, semi-quick-drying red-lead paint which is an easy brushing material suitable for general use and dries in 24 hours; and type III, red-lead paint in a varnish vehicle which dries within 8 hours and may be used for touch-up work on clean smooth steel.

Zinc-dust primers have good rust-inhibitive properties and are particularly effective for galvanized iron and sheet zinc. While the primary function of these paints is to provide adequate adherence on galvanized metal, they are also satisfactory as finish paints and may be used in one or more coats.

Quick-drying metal primers for home workshop machinery and automobiles are iron-oxide primers in which the vehicle is a thin varnish. They dry to a smooth velvety, flat eggshell finish, and give excellent foundations for decorative coats.

As finish coats on iron or steel, black and dark-colored paints are more durable than light-tinted paints. Red-lead paint should not be used as a final coat, since it does not retain its color. One of the best finish coats

1695

for metal is aluminum paint made by mixing about 2 lbs. of aluminum powder or paste with 1 gallon of spar varnish.

Copper

Copper gutters and flashings, as well as copper or bronze screening, may cause yellowish-green stains on light- or white-painted houses. One way to avoid this is to paint or varnish the copper or bronze. The surface of the metal should be cleaned by washing with gasoline or turpentine, and a priming coat composed of 1½ to 2 lbs. of aluminum powder to 1 gallon of aluminum mixing varnish applied, followed by the desired color coat. Weathered copper or bronze fly-screening should be dusted and then given two coats of thin black enamel. Zinc dust-zinc oxide paints may also be used on copper and bronze if a gray color is acceptable.

10 Steps to Successful Outdoor Painting

Check exterior wood siding and wood trim for loose paint. You can remove small areas with sandpaper and sanding block.

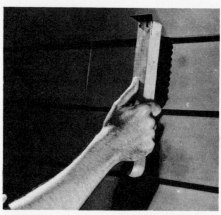

A wire brush comes in handy to remove any grime and surface dirt before applying the paint.

1696

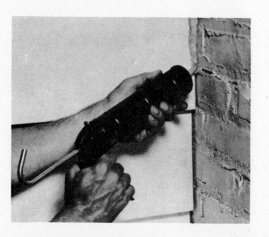

Photographs courtesy of PPG Industries

Where necessary, calk joints around windows, doors and chimneys. You can do this with a putty knife and calking compound or it's easier and quicker to do a better job with a calking gun. (above left) See **Calking**. Check around the window panes for loose putty. If any is missing or loose, replace it with sound putty. (above right) See **Glazing**.

Start painting on the outside at the highest part of the house. Make certain that the ladder is secure before you climb it. See **Ladders.**

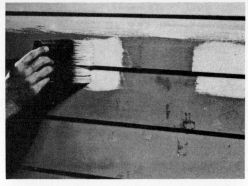

Lay brushload of paint on in two or three places and then brush out well. Note that you never soak the entire brush in paint; do not get ferrule wet.

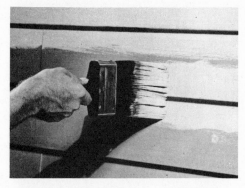

When painting clapboard or beveled or shiplap siding, always paint the edges first, using the brush on its flat side, never its edge. You can do the same job with special rollers.

After brushing out the paint, finish with tips of the brush to a thin feather-edge. Now continue to lay on brushloads of paint, working from the wet edge outward.

When painting around window sash outside the house, keep the sash brush well loaded for full-bodied stroke. In this way, you will be able to do a better job with less smearing of paint on the glass.

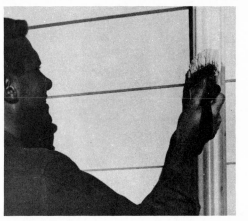

If the surface coat of gutters and downspouts is still good, you can apply the final coat immediately. Otherwise, it is essential that a prime coat be applied before the final coat.

1697

Painting—Interior

Interior painting requires as careful preparation of surfaces as does exterior painting. The advent of odorless paints now makes it possible to paint any time of the year. Formerly, most interior painting in the home was done in the fall or spring, when it was possible to leave the windows open to ventilate the room. But open windows brought dust into the room to mar the finished painted surface.

A good interior paint job is often 50% preparation and 50% painting. Do not rush in preparing the surfaces in your eagerness to get at the brush or roller. If you do not prepare the surfaces properly, you'll be back with the paint brush or roller in a few months.

It is recommended that you re-read the section on *PAINTING—BASIC PREPARATION OF THE SURFACES*. Then, in this section you will find the necessary information on the application of different types of paints on various interior wall, ceiling and floor materials.

Plaster

New dry plaster in good condition, which is to be finished with a paint other than water paint, should be given a coat of primer-sealer and allowed to dry thoroughly before being inspected for uniformity of appearance. Variations in gloss and color differences in the case of tinted primers indicate whether or not the whole surface has been completely sealed. If not, a second coat of primer-sealer should be applied. If only a few "suction spots" are apparent, a second coat over these areas may be sufficient.

1698

PAINTING POINTERS

Avoid a ring of paint where you put down can by keeping a paper plate under it. Daub a little paint on the bottom of can, press the plate against it and it will stick.

Unpainted furniture should first be sealed by brushing a very thin wash coat of shellac on the raw wood. When dry, smooth lightly with sandpaper. Apply undercoat, brush out thoroughly, let dry at least 24 hours and sand again. Apply finish coat with smooth, light brush strokes, using just the tip of the bristles.

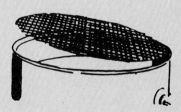

Fit a disk of window screening inside can after mixing paint well. As the screen sinks, it will carry lumpy paint particles to bottom.

PAINTING POINTERS

Angle your brush into corners; never paint with its sides. Angling in protects the bristles and gives you a smoother, more even finish.

You can lengthen the life of a fine, pure bristle brush by using it only to apply finish coats. Keep brushes with synthetic or mixed bristles handy for priming and for use on rough surfaces that wear down bristles fast.

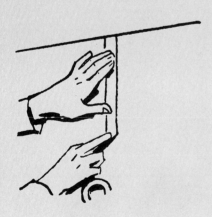

Use masking tape where two shades are to meet. Paint on one color, let it dry, apply tape at the dividing line and then brush on the second color. The result will be a neater job and you'll save time.

A flat, semigloss, or high-gloss finish may be applied to the primed surface. For a flat finish, two coats of flat wall paint should follow the priming coat. For a semi-gloss finish, one coat of flat wall paint and one coat of semi-gloss paint should be applied to the primed surface. For a high-gloss finish, one coat of semi-gloss paint and one coat of high-gloss enamel should be used over the priming coat.

Before applying water paints of the calcimine type to new plastered walls they should be sized, using either a glue-water size or, if the plaster is dry, a thin varnish or primer-sealer. Cold water paints of the casein type may be applied either directly to a plastered surface, or the surface may be first given a coat of primer-sealer to equalize uneven suction effects. The same is true of resin-emulsion paints, with the recommendations of the manufacturer of the product being given preference in case of doubt. Since resin-emulsion paints usually contain some oil in the binder, they should ordinarily be applied only to plaster which has dried thoroughly.

Texture wall paints may also be used on plaster surfaces. The advantages of this type of paint are that one coat economically produces a textured decoration and relieves the monotony of smooth flat paint. It also covers cracks or patches in the plaster more completely than ordinary wall paint. The disadvantages of texture wall paint are that they collect dust and are difficult to restore to a smooth finish. These materials are available as water- or oil-base paints, are thicker than ordinary wall paints, and may be applied to wallboard as

1699

well as plaster to produce textured effects such as random, Spanish, mission, and multicolored.

For more information, see the section on *PLASTER*.

Composition Wallboard

Composition wallboard usually presents no particular painting difficulties if the ordinary precautions are observed, such as making certain that the surface is dry and free from grease and oil. The painting procedure for wallboard is the same as for plaster; it requires a priming and sealing coat followed by whatever finish coats are desired, or may be given one-coat flat or resin-emulsion type paint.

Wallpaper

Water-thinned paint may be applied to wallpaper that is well-bonded to the wall and does not contain dyes which may bleed into the paint. One thickness of wallpaper is preferable for paint application. Paints other than those of the water-thinned type may also be applied to wallpaper by following the directions given for painting plaster. However, wallpaper coated with such a paint is difficult to remove without injury to the plaster.

Wood Walls and Trim

1700

New interior walls and wood trim should be smoothed with sandpaper and dusted before painting or varnishing. To preserve the grain of the wood, the surface may be rubbed with linseed oil, varnished or shellacked, and waxed. If an opaque finish is desired, semi-gloss paint thinned with 1 pint of turpentine per gallon of paint or the primer-sealer previously described for walls may be

used as a priming coat on wood. One or two coats of semi-gloss paint should then be applied over the thoroughly dry prime coat, or if a full-gloss finish is desired, the last coat should be a high-gloss enamel.

Wood Floor Finishes

For information on varnishing wood floors, refer to the section on *FLOORS, WOOD—FINISHING*.

Masonry Walls and Ceilings

Interior masonry walls and ceilings above grade may, in general, be painted in much the same manner as plaster surfaces. Here again, it is necessary to allow adequate time for the masonry to dry before applying paint and, in addition, attention should be given to the preparation of the surface. When decorating a wall containing Portland cement (concrete, for example), it is essential to take precautions against the attack of alkali. For this purpose, alkali-resist-

Easy way to avoid cleaning the tray afterwards is to line it with aluminum foil before you pour the paint into it. Use a fairly thick piece of foil or several sheets of the household type.

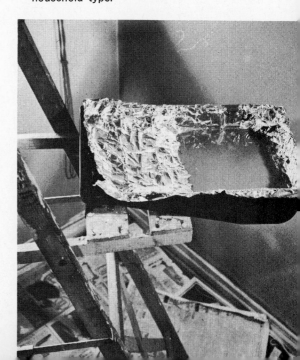

ant primers such as rubber-base paints may be used when oil paints are to follow.

Cement-water paints are best suited for application to basement walls which are damp as a result of leakage or condensation. To apply these paints, the same procedure should be followed as is described here for painting exterior masonry walls.

Concrete Floors

Two general types of paints for concrete floors are varnish and rubber-base paint. Each has its limitations and the finish cannot be patched without the patched area showing through. Floor and deck enamel of the varnish type gives good service on concrete floors above grade where there is no moisture present.

Rubber-base paints, which dry to a hard semi-gloss finish, may be used on concrete floors below grade, providing the floor is not continually damp from seepage and condensation.

Paint should not be applied to a concrete basement floor until the concrete has aged for at least a year. The floor should be dry when painted, the best time for application being during the winter or early spring (assuming there is some heating apparatus in the basement), when the humidity in the basement is low. In general, three coats of paint are required on an unpainted floor, and the first coat should be thin to secure good penetration. After the paint is dry, it should be protected with a coat of floor wax.

In repainting concrete floors, where the existing paint has been waxed and is in good condition except for some worn areas, the surface

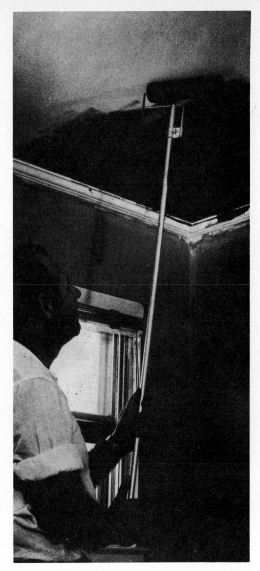

Photographs courtesy of E Z Paintr Corp.

No more standing on a plank in the air or climbing up and down a ladder to paint a ceiling. A convenient extension handle is attached to the ordinary roller. It makes it easy to reach the ceiling while standing on the floor.

1701

should be scrubbed with cloths saturated with turpentine or petroleum spirits and rubbed with steel wool while wet, to remove all wax before repainting. If this is not done, the paint will not adhere and dry satis-

For a stippled effect, you can use a roller with a special cover that will produce the stipple effect with enamel paint. Here, a stipple coat is being applied over glass.

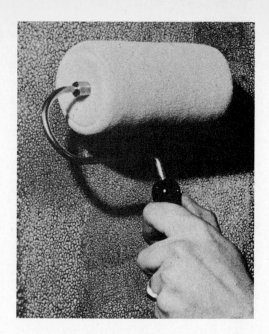

Getting into corners is always a problem! Working a brush into a corner may result in splashed and spattered paint. An ordinary roller just won't get all the way in. The "doughnut" is just the right answer.
Photographs courtesy of E Z Paintr Corp.

1702

factorily. If the old paint is badly worn, it should be removed by treating with a solution of 2 lbs. of caustic soda (household lye) to 1 gallon of hot water. This may be mopped on the surface and allowed to remain for 30 minutes after which the floor can be washed with hot water and scraped with a wide steel scraper. Another method of application is to spread a thin layer of sawdust, which has been soaked in caustic solution over the floor and allow it to stand overnight. The following morning, the floor can be washed with hot water and the paint scraped off. The surface should then be rinsed thoroughly with clean water.

If rubber-base paint has been used, the caustic soda treatment may not be effective and it may be necessary to use an organic solvent type of paint remover.

Caution:—When using caustic soda or lye, avoid splashing eyes, skin, and clothing.

Interior Metal

Interior metal, such as heating grilles, radiators, and exposed water pipes, should be painted to prevent rust and to make them as inconspicuous as possible. New metal should be cleaned of grease and dirt by washing with mineral spirits, and any rust should be removed by sanding, after which a metal primer should be applied. The finish coat may be either a flat wall paint or a semi-gloss enamel.

If you are not sure of the primer to use on metal, the paint dealer or manufacturer will give you this information, dependent on the type of metal to be painted.

Usually on exposed air ducts of galvanized metal a primer coat of zinc dust-zinc oxide paint is used, before the finish coat is applied.

The paints may be applied by brush or spray; the small spray attachment for vacuum cleaners is very convenient, especially for painting radiators.

Brass lighting fixtures and andirons may be polished and kept bright by coating with metal lacquers. The lacquers, held in cans under pressure, may be sprayed directly from the container. Old-fashioned or unattractive lighting fixtures may be painted with ceiling or wall paint to harmonize with the surrounding surfaces.

Special Surfaces

WHITEWASH

Whitewashes and lime paints must be thin when applied. In fact, best results will be obtained if the application is so thin that the surface to which it is applied may easily be seen through the film while it is wet. The coating will dry opaque, but two thin coats will give better results than one thick coat.

A large whitewash brush is best for applying the wash. One should not attempt to brush out the coating, as in applying oil paint, but simply spread the whitewash on as evenly and quickly as possible.

The principal ingredient in whitewash is lime paste. A satisfactory paste can be made with hydrated lime, but better results are obtained by using quicklime paste that has been slaked with enough water to make it moderately stiff. The lime paste should be kept in a loosely covered container for at least several days. Eight gallons of stiff lime paste can be made by slaking 25 lbs. of quicklime in 10 gallons of water, or by soaking 50 lbs. of hydrated lime in 6 gallons of water. After soaking, the paste should be strained through a fine screen to remove lumps or foreign matter.

Whitewash can be made from various combinations of lime paste and other ingredients. The following two formulas are satisfactory.

Formula No. 1

Casein . . . . 5 lbs.
Trisodium Phosphate . 3 lbs.
Lime paste . . . . 8 gals.

The casein, which serves as the glue binder, should be soaked in 2 gallons of hot water until thoroughly

1703

When painting an entire room, start your painting job with the ceiling. When painting a ceiling always work across the narrow dimension.

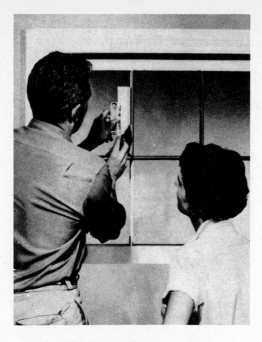

Paint shields are helpful in keeping paint off the glass when painting the sash.

A paint shield also comes in handy when painting the baseboard molding or the bottom of a door. It protects the floor.

softened, which should be approximately 2 hours. After dissolving the trisodium phosphate in 1 gallon of water it should be added to the casein, stirring the mixture until the casein dissolves. This solution should be mixed with the lime paste and 3 gallons of water.

Formula No. 2

Common salt	12 lbs.
Powdered alum	6 lbs.
Molasses	1 qt.
Lime paste	8 gals.

The salt and alum should be dissolved in 4 gallons of hot water, after which the molasses may be added to the mixture. The resulting clear solution is then added to the lime paste, stirred vigorously, and thinned with water to the desired consistency. This whitewash has a yellow tinge when first applied, but the color disappears in a few days leaving a white film.

Another satisfactory whitewash can be made by diluting a moderately heavy cold lime paste (about 33 lbs. of hydrated lime and 8 gallons of water) with 5 gallons of skim-milk.

The area covered by a gallon of whitewash depends upon the nature of the surface, but ordinarily a gallon will cover about 225 sq. ft. on wood, about 180 sq. ft. on brick, and about 270 sq. ft. on plaster. The formulas mentioned will make from 10 to 14 gallons of whitewash. If a smaller quantity is desired, the amount of each ingredient should be reduced proportionately.

STIPPLING

Whether you desire the effect of stippling (tiny paint dots) as a decorative effect, or if you have a wall

If painting the panels with enamel, smooth the surface with light, upward strokes, using a brush that is almost dry.

When painting a panel door, always paint the insides of the panels first with horizontal strokes.

which has an uneven surface and you feel you can hide the defect by stippling it, you may accomplish this result very simply.

For stippling you need a special brush; get one that is flat, and has short, stiff bristles.

The first step is to cover the surface with a coat of paint, using your regular paint brush, or spray, or roller. Then, while the surface is still wet, take the dry stipple brush and energetically with short strokes drive the ends or the bristles into the wet paint. Be sure not to brush across. The result will be clusters of dots. Every few minutes wipe the brush with a cloth, to keep the bristle ends clean and dry.

Painting—

Miscellaneous Surfaces

Porcelain

Surfaces in this category, which for this purpose may include sinks, bathtubs, porcelainized steel as is found on ranges, laundry equipment, refrigerators and the like, often become chipped by objects which have dropped on them. An ugly marred surface is the result.

Epoxy paints of the proper tint can be used to repair these damages. Or they may even be used to change the color of the appliance in question. As always, when working with this material, it must be applied to a spotless, grease-free surface if it is expected to adhere properly.

In repairing chips or nicks, apply several coats of epoxy until the indentation is filled up level with the surrounding surface.

Awnings and Deck Chairs

Faded or discolored awnings where the canvas is in good condi-

1705

tion may be freshened by coating with awning paints which are available at most paint and hardware stores in a variety of nonfading colors. These materials are easily applied with a brush, are nonpenetrating, and dry to a smooth flat flexible finish. They may also be used to renew the color of old canvas on deck chairs, lawn umbrellas, or glider cushions.

Porch Decks

Exposed canvas porch decks are difficult to maintain, but may be painted with porch and deck enamel or aluminum paint. The coating should be renewed annually if the deck is to remain leakproof. Porch and deck enamel produces a glossy

Faded canvas on awnings and deck chairs can be renewed with special paint if the canvas is in good condition.

finish; and aluminum paint a silvery metallic finish.

Doors

In painting a door, the type of wood, the severity of exposure, the finish and color desired, and the type of paint should all be taken into consideration. When applying each coat of paint, finish the panels first, the center rail next, then the top and bottom rails, next the vertical stiles, and finally the edges. If the surface is kept smooth by rubbing with sandpaper between each coat, the door should present a smooth velvetlike appearance when finished.

Windows

Before painting a window sash, be sure to scrape off all the old, loose putty and coat the wood recesses with linseed oil before applying the new putty. A shield cut from a piece of tin will speed the work of painting by protecting the glass from "run overs" while still permitting enough paint to flow on to the muntins or sash bars to give a good seal between the wood and glass. The muntins or sash bars should be painted first, then the stiles and rails of the sash, next the window frames and trim and, finally, the sill and apron below.

Screens

Door and window screens will last longer and look better if kept well painted. For this, special screen paints are best, but they should be thinned to avoid clogging the mesh. A coat of thinned white paint applied to the screen wire makes the interior of the house less visible from the outside.

How to Glaze and Paint Wood Sash

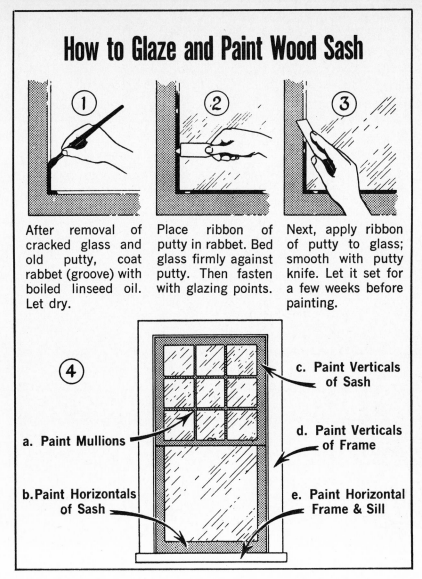

After removal of cracked glass and old putty, coat rabbet (groove) with boiled linseed oil. Let dry.

Place ribbon of putty in rabbet. Bed glass firmly against putty. Then fasten with glazing points.

Next, apply ribbon of putty to glass; smooth with putty knife. Let it set for a few weeks before painting.

a. Paint Mullions

b. Paint Horizontals of Sash

c. Paint Verticals of Sash

d. Paint Verticals of Frame

e. Paint Horizontal Frame & Sill

Painting window sash is not at all difficult. Apply the paint with a small varnish brush or a flat or oval sash tool. Start with the mullions and continue as the arrows indicate. If there are paint spatters on the glass when you have finished, remove them with a razor blade soon after the paint dries.

The necessary tools and materials are a screen paint applicator and bristle brush; special screen paint, spar varnish, or enamel in desired color and small amount of boiled linseed oil or turpentine for thinning.

A cheap grade of screen wire will probably require painting every year, while galvanized wire may show signs of rust only after long use and may then require only a light coat of paint. Copper or bronze screen wire will not deteriorate if not painted, but the corrosion products resulting from weathering make it advisable either to paint or varnish copper or bronze screens to avoid staining the trim and outside walls of a house. If it is desirable to retain the original copper or bronze color of the screens, a high-grade spar varnish should be applied in two coats to both sides of the screen cloth. Inasmuch as this will not last as long

1707

as the enamel, the screens will need to be coated with spar varnish at least every other season. If a dark color is not objectionable, a coat of black enamel should last several seasons.

Paint may be applied evenly and economically to screens with a special screen applicator. Most paint dealers carry these applicators but, if not available, they are not difficult to make. A block of wood 1″x3″x8″ may be covered with thick felt or carpet attached to the face side of the block with the nap outward. A cleat of wood for a handle should be nailed along the center of the opposite side of the block. The carpet may be fastened by glue or tacks but if tacks or brads are used, the heads should be well embedded so that they will not catch on the wire mesh while the paint is being applied.

The screen should be placed on a level surface like a table top, and cleaned of all dust, soot, and loose rust with a bristle brush. If more thorough cleaning is necessary, the screen may be washed with soap and warm water applied with a brush, rinsed with clear water, and dried with a cloth. After the screen has been cleaned on both sides and dried thoroughly, paint may be applied by brushing the face of the applicator with a moderate amount of paint and spreading the paint over the screen with the applicator. In this way, the screen may be painted quite rapidly and easily with a thin even coating without clogging the mesh.

The frames should not require painting oftener than once in every 3 to 5 years. If the screening is cleaned and painted once a year as

1708

described, its life will be prolonged and the screens will present a neat appearance.

Swimming Pools

Vitreous tile is the preferred coating for swimming pool wall and floor surfaces, but there are three general types of paint which may be used as decorative finishes: cement-water paints, enamel paints with water-resisting varnish vehicle, and waterproof enamel paints. These paints are available in appropriate light blue and light green colors.

The advantages of cement-water paints are their ease of application and low cost; their disadvantages are their tendency to absorb body oils and grease and to accumulate algae when it exists. One season is the maximum period that wall and floor surfaces of a much-used pool coated

A deep luster can be obtained and the color of the wood preserved by applying a protective surface coat over either interior or exterior wood furniture. This final coat can be brushed on or, if you have the equipment, sprayed on.

Photograph courtesy of Monsanto Chemical Co.

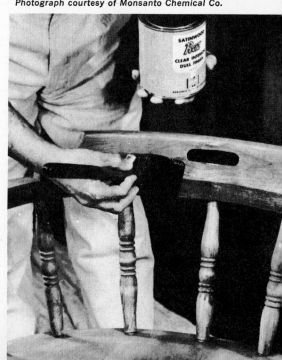

with cement-water paints can be kept in good condition without re-painting.

Enamel paints must be applied only to clean surfaces and no water should be put into the pool for several days after the application of each coat. Enamel paints give a smooth attractive surface that may last for a season, but may develop blisters and peel during that time.

Waterproof enamel paints will probably give the least trouble since they dry to a smooth hard-gloss finish and are chemically resistant to moisture and water-purifying agents.

Wood Furniture

For information on various finishes—refer to the section on *FURNITURE FINISHING*.

Baby Furniture

Furniture with which the baby comes into contact must be finished with a non-poisonous paint, especially if the child has a tendency to lick, taste, and chew everything within reach. Buy special baby enamel, which comes in pretty colors and is washable. This applies to painted toys, too.

Painting—Spraying Techniques

Applying paint with a sprayer is faster than with either a brush or a roller, but you'll need more experience in handling this "tool" than either the brush or roller to produce a satisfactory job.

Spray painting can be done in a variety of ways:

Guns having internal-mix nozzles generally have three interchangeable nozzles to produce different types of patterns. The 45° nozzle is very useful for spraying floors or ceilings, since you can paint at an angle without tipping the gun.

The overshot type of external-mix nozzles produce a round pattern, while the other external-mix nozzles produce a fan-shaped pattern. The higher-priced guns of this type usually are made with a built-in spray-pattern adjustment to vary the pattern from round to fan-shaped—the one nozzle serves all purposes.

1. You can use the simple spray attachment that usually comes with a vacuum cleaner, particularly the tank-type cleaner. However, the air pressure is low and this type of sprayer works best on thin liquids. This sprayer has an elementary control and is not suitable for fine lacquer or precision spraying.

2. You can purchase pressurized-aerosol cans with different types of paints in a variety of colors. This technique works fine for touch-up painting, especially on appliances. However, because of the limited amount of paint held by the pressurized can, this is a costly method for painting large areas.

1709

MATERIAL
NEEDLE VALVE

BODY

AIR-CONTROL SCREW
ADJUSTS WIDTH OF SPRAY

AIR
NOZZLE

MATERIAL
NOZZLE

MATERIAL
HOSE
CONNECTION

AIR-VALVE
ASSEMBLY

CONTROL SCREW
FOR REGULATING FLOW
OF MATERIAL AND FOR
REMOVING NEEDLE
VALVE

TWO-FINGER TRIGGER

AIR
PASSAGE

GRIP

AIR-HOSE
CONNECTION

DEVILBISS

Cross-section view of spray gun.

1710

3. Inexpensive vibrator-type sprayer guns are available and they are considerably better than the attachments made for vacuum cleaners. However, they vary in the quality of performance and some cannot be used for really efficient spray painting. Others, however, are satisfactory and work well with most types of paints.

4. Sprayers of the diaphragm type or working off a compressor are the more professional tools to use for spraying. These are more expensive than the vibrator type and, on the average, perform more efficiently than the vibrator type.

Selecting the Sprayer

You can paint about four to six times faster with a sprayer than with any other painting tool. When you select a paint sprayer, you should be guided by the following factors:

1. Capacity—how much will the sprayer hold? Can it be used with all types of paints or only certain ones?

2. What is its speed—how much paint can it deliver per minute?

3. What are its design qualities—

is it convenient to handle? Is it easy to operate? Can you clean it easily? Does it have interchangeable nozzles?

While these are the primary factors to consider, you should also examine the use of sprayers:

1. Type of air supply

• Bleeder-type guns are designed for direct connection of the gun to the compressor so that the air is blowing through the sprayer at all times. The trigger action is used only to control the flow of the paint through the gun.

• Non-bleeder guns operate with the trigger shutting off both the air supply and the paint. They cannot be used with continually running compressors since shutting off the air flow at the gun would result in the bursting of the air supply line or blowing the safety valve on the compressor.

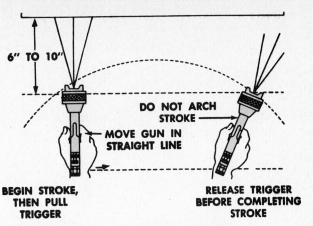

6" TO 10"

DO NOT ARCH STROKE

MOVE GUN IN STRAIGHT LINE

BEGIN STROKE, THEN PULL TRIGGER

RELEASE TRIGGER BEFORE COMPLETING STROKE

Proper way to spray a surface—begin the stroke and then pull the trigger, continuing to move your hand in a straight line. Release pressure on the trigger and stop spraying before you complete the stroke.

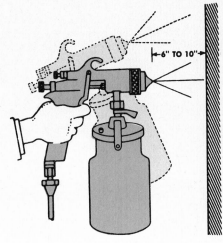

6" TO 10"

Spray gun should be held perpendicular to the surface. If held at an angle, there will be an uneven deposit of paint.

2. Paint feed to the nozzle

• Pressure-fed guns have an airtight cup to hold the paint. Air pressure on the top of the paint forces it up to the gun nozzle.

• Syphon guns depend upon suction to lift the paint from the cup or

1711

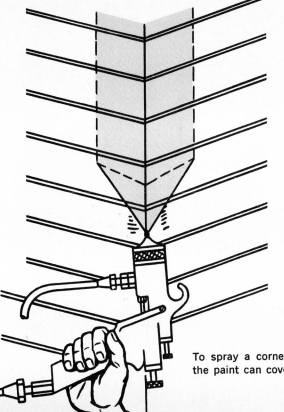

To spray a corner, hold the gun so that the paint can cover both sides at once.

Spray guns come in various shapes and sizes. This model with an adjustable nozzle can be used with paint in the large aluminum can.

mixing of the heavier paints used with a spray gun.

• External-mix nozzles atomize the paint in air jets outside the nozzle. This type is best used with lighter paints and quick-drying paints which might otherwise tend to clog the nozzle.

Basic Preparation

Before starting to spray, the surface should be thoroughly cleaned and all rough spots smoothed with sandpaper and wiped free of dust. Everything in a room that might be marred by settling spray should be covered with old sheets or dropcloths.

Before starting to spray, door knobs, wall switches, and light fixtures should be covered with masking tape which can be obtained in paint and hardware stores in widths from ½″ up.

Masking tape should also be laid along the frames of windows and mirrors. The glass should be coated with masking compound which may be obtained from paint and automotive supply stores. In bathrooms, use tape and newspapers to mask tub, lavatory and toilet.

If masking is not feasible, a piece of metal or stiff cardboard may be used as a shield, moving it

container into the air stream at the outlet of the nozzle.

3. How the paint is atomized for spraying

• Internal-mix nozzles atomize the paint in a mixing chamber inside the nozzle. This provides for a better

1712

TYPE OF MATERIAL	TYPE OF FEED REQUIRED			TYPE OF NOZZLE REQUIRED		
	Pressure	Syphon	Either	Internal Mix	External Mix	Either
Enamel			x			x
Lacquer			x		x	
Shellac	x				x	
Stain			x			x
Undercoat	x			x		
Water Paint			x			x
Oil Paint	x			x		
Synthetic Paint			x			x

along as the spraying proceeds. This is a convenient way to separately spray screen wire and screen frames.

All paint materials used in a spray gun should be strained through a clean, relatively lint-free cloth before using.

Spraying With a Gun

When spraying paint, always wear a respirator. It gives valuable protection against paint poisoning and should be worn even for outdoor work with a cap to keep drift spray out of the hair. Do not smoke while spraying. (If the respirator is worn, this will be impossible.) Also make sure that ventilation is adequate for health as well as fire safety. Never spray near an open flame, or where there is a possibility of sparks flying, as spraying mixes paint and air to an explosive proportion. When painting indoors, always have the windows open wide; never spray in a closed room unless an exhaust fan is in operation that will change the air every 3 minutes.

Before actual painting operations are started, adjust the gun and practice spraying on scrap material to obtain the proper flow of paint. Hold the gun in one hand and with the other keep the hose clear of the surface that is being sprayed. The spray tip should be held 6″ to 10″ from the surface to which the paint is being applied.

If a large panel or wall is being

Paint in spray cans is the biggest boon ever for small touch up or repainting jobs. The spray pattern is easily controlled so most overspray can be avoided. Here spray can is being used to renew an attractive wicker basket.

Photo courtesy of Valspar Paints

1713

Even metallic paints are packaged in spray cans. Finishes of this type are especially useful in restoring worn lamps and other household items with metal surfaces.

Two strips of masking tape to define the area to be painted and a couple of bursts from your trusty spray can, and you've put an indelible identifying mark on your garden tools. Borrowing neighbors will be constantly reminded whose they are. Use bright colors.

The versatility of aerosol paint knows no bounds. There's no better way to do an accurate neat job of striping in conjunction with masking tape.

Another use for which you can't beat spray cans is in automobile touchup. Of course, you must make sure you're getting a matching color, or the repair will look worse than the original.

Photo courtesy Plasti-Kote

sprayed, begin at the upper corner and work from right to left. Move down as each swath is laid on. Since the center half of the last sprayed strip gets the thickest coat, lap the upper fourth of each new stroke over the lower fourth of the preceding stroke.

On each stroke, begin swinging the gun from a point to one side of where the spray is to begin. When the starting point is reached, press the trigger and hold it until the other edge of the panel sweep is reached.

Always sweep the spray stroke so that the tip of the gun stays the same distance from the surface and so that the spray will strike at right angles. The pace of the stroke should not change. Any hesitation or halt without releasing the trigger will let too much paint pile up, and a sag or run will result.

Holding the gun too close to the work will also produce a sag or run, and holding it too far away will fog the finish and produce a dull effect. Meeting points of the surfaces, such as corners and sharp edges, are spots that tend to catch too much paint and are sprayed best with short successive spurts, aiming the gun so that each spurt is at right angles to the nearest surface. This technique applies to any finish.

A few specific suggestions follow:

1. In spraying paint, varnish, and enamel, the material should first be thinned in accordance with the manufacturer's instructions.

2. The first coat should then be "fogged" on, holding the gun a little further from the surface than the suggested 6″ to 10″.

3. One coat of primer and one coat of finish may cover a surface, but two finish coats are better.

4. Allow the paint to dry thoroughly between coats, and on small objects a better finish is obtained if the surface is lightly sanded between coats.

Lacquers are rather thin materials which dry very rapidly. They should be applied in three to five coats, using the thinner recommended by the manufacturer. Lacquer cannot as a rule be successfully applied over paints, varnish, or enamel.

Among the common faults in spray finishes are sags (finish laid on so thick that it flows downward in drapes); runs (longer drops streaking down, usually from sags); holidays (spots left bare); orange peeling (bumpy finish); and fogging (dull, pebbled finish usually resulting from the gun being held too far from the surface).

Partition Wall

Walls within the house are divided into two types—partition and bearing. Partition walls are "non-bearing" —that is, they do not bear any load as compared with a bearing wall which supports some weight. The bearing walls run at right angles to the joists above and support them.

Removing a Partition Wall

The average homeowner can remove a partition wall in his home without endangering the house structure. Removing a bearing wall, however, is a more complicated

1715

This is a bearing wall.

1716

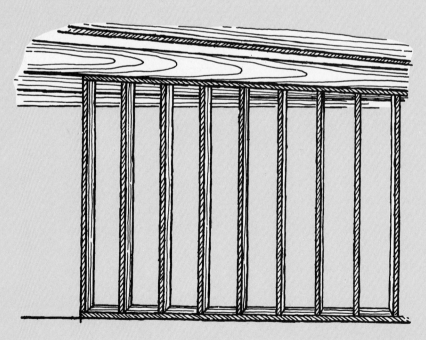

This is a partition wall.

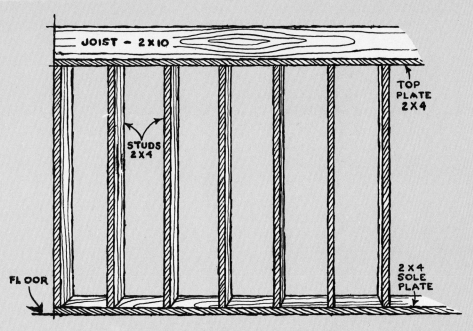

JOIST - 2X10

STUDS 2X4

TOP PLATE 2X4

FLOOR

2 X 4 SOLE PLATE

Conventional method of framing a partition wall.

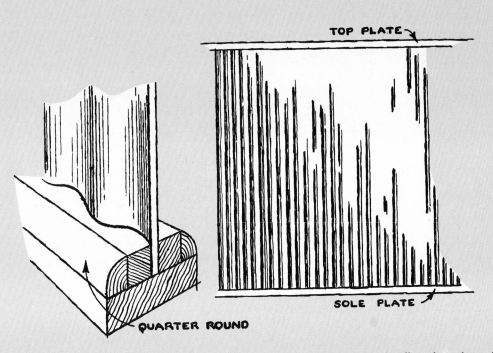

TOP PLATE

QUARTER ROUND

SOLE PLATE

1717

Single wall material partition wall can be made of corrugated fiberglass, hardboard or plywood. Use at least ½″ thickness of the latter two.

process and ordinarily should not be undertaken by the average homeowner. On the other hand, the more advanced handyman, who knows how to prop up the structure, can remove a bearing wall and replace it with a beam without endangering the house itself.

The partition wall normally runs parallel to the joist above. If you have any doubts about whether the wall is a partition or bearing wall, it is best to check with a local architect or builder. Another check you should make before attempting to remove a partition wall is for pipes running through the wall. While it is possible to shift pipes, this often involves considerable plumbing work and may be too much for the average homeowner. To remove a partition wall, you should:

1. Pry off the baseboard molding and ceiling trim on both sides of the wall.

2. Shut off the electrical power to any lines in the wall. With the fuse removed or the main switch off, disconnect the electrical lines within the wall from either the basement or attic.

3. Break the wall material between any two studs and start to remove the old wall material. If you have plaster walls, it is necessary to chop the plaster out with a hammer and possibly a cold chisel. With wallboard, you can pry the panels loose. If you have wood walls, you may wish to remove the pieces with the least amount of damage. In that case, pry the boards loose along the sole and top plates and pull the nails out.

4. Remove the loose electrical wires from between the studs as well

as any outlet boxes or wall fixture boxes.

5. To remove the studs, you may have to cut each one and pry them loose separately. In some cases, careful hammering will enable you to withdraw them uncut from between the sole and top plates.

6. Remove the sole and top plates by prying loose with a crowbar.

7. After all the partition wall sections have been removed, it will be necessary to patch the ceiling, walls and floor to provide a continuous surface between the two rooms joined.

How to Install a Partition Wall

If you wish to divide a large room into two with a partition wall, you can do so in several different ways. One is the conventional way of installing plates and studs and covering each side with wall material. However, you can use glass block, corrugated fiberglass plastic panels, or single hardboard or wood panels.

To follow the conventional method, nail a 2x3 or 2x4 sole plate to the floor and a top plate to the ceiling. Cut 2x3 or 2x4 studs to fit between the plates and toe-nail them into position. If it is necessary to add a door, see section on *DOOR FRAMING*. After the plates and studs, either 16″ or 24″ on center, are in place, apply the wall material to each side. To conceal the joint between the wall and floor, add a baseboard.

To use a single wall material, such as corrugated fiberglass, hardboard or plywood, you can use a 1x3 for the sole and plates. The wall material is set between the plates and held in place with cleats attached to the plates on each side of the material. You can use any square stock and finish the outside edge by attaching a piece of half-round as shown in the sketch.

Patio

While the dictionary defines a patio as an enclosed court, it has come to be used to describe a terrace alongside the house, a barbecue-play area with a roof, a three-wall and roofed shelter away from the house or a slab of concrete abutting the house. In many regions, the patio exists under a local name.

Here, we have used the term *patio* to describe an outdoor living area. It can be raised off the ground or flush with it. It can be sheltered with a wall or two and a roof, or exposed with but a few shrubs and trees to block the sun. It can be a sun porch, a lanai or a barbecue shelter.

Planning the Patio

Whether you are planning to build an outdoor recreation area or hope to modify your existing one, there are certain basic elements which are essential in good patio planning. One of the most important is the orientation of the patio, particularly in relation to the sun.

Merely building your patio in the back of your house so that it is sheltered from the street is a poor solution to the location problem. There are ways to have your patio face the street and yet have that needed privacy. Your first job is to

Pots of bright nasturtiums with ivy create a half-enclosure for an outdoor table on this concrete patio, setting it off from the pool and surrounding areas.

The "groaning board," outdoor style, greets visitors to this delightful backyard living room.

decide upon the positioning of your patio in relation to the sun.

South—A patio that faces the south always has the sun, practically from sunrise to sunset. Provisions must be made to keep the sun's rays from beating down and heating the patio. A roof is a must. Some means of shielding the patio from the setting sun must also be found.

Photograph courtesy of Manor Crafts.

Which way does your patio face? West patios are hot; north patios are cold. For a decorative touch, and as a means of orientation, you can embed an attractive brass compass in your patio pavement. These compasses come in many styles and are made of ¼″ cast brass. They can be installed in any surface as they have spurs on the back for bonding.

1720

West—A patio facing the west is a hot patio for it receives the full force of the sun from early afternoon until the sun sets late in the evening during the summer. Overhead protection is a must as is some means of blocking the setting sun's

rays in the late afternoon and evening.

East—Although the sun shines directly on the patio in the morning, an east patio cools off later in the day and the house blocks the sun from early afternoon on. An east patio is desirable in hot climates and, unless you wish protection from rain, there is little need for any overhead covering.

North—Facing the north, a patio receives only the very early sun and then is protected by the house for the remainder of the day. In some areas, the late setting sun may shine on the patio, but by that time the heat is gone. In other areas, where the evening turns cool, some provision for heating the outdoor living area must be provided for comfort on a north patio.

Basic Ingredients of an Attractive Patio

While orientation is of primary importance in planning a patio, there are many other factors which you should consider. No one factor makes a patio good or bad; it is a combination that does the trick. Here are some of the elements necessary to make a patio attractive and functional.

1. The patio should be oriented to invite or block out the sun, depending upon your location and what you require.

2. A well-planned patio is part of the house; it is not just an addition! Your patio design should blend in with your home's over-all design and architecture.

3. A "room" outdoors must be bigger than one inside the home. Provide adequate space for the larger-

Patios shown here appear completely different yet are closely related. Both are made of masonry loose-laid on a sand bed. (Top) Large concrete blocks poured in simple homemade forms have been laid with 4″ between them. This permits the growth of grass for a naturalistic look. An evergreen ground cover can also be planted. (Below) Concrete patio blocks sold by many building supply yards measure about 2″ thick x 8″ x 16″. These are butted tightly together and crevices filled with clean builder's sand broomed in.

Photos courtesy Portland Cement Association

1721

This wood deck consists of 4'x4' modules made by cutting a 4'x8' sheet of ½" exterior-grade DFPA plywood in half and nailing 4' lengths of 2x4 to the plywood. The modules are placed on a lumber gridwork. They are movable and can be repositioned to create a variety of surface patterns. Or they can be left out to create openings for planters, a fire pit or barbecue.

sized furniture and leave plenty of space for "breathing."

4. Add to the take-it-easy atmosphere outdoors by providing comfortable furniture for dining and relaxing.

5. Your patio should blend in with your landscaping and garden planning.

6. Privacy outdoors can be gained partly by orientation of the patio and partly by the use of fences and shields.

7. Controlling the weather can be achieved by adding a roof to keep off the hot sun or to provide a sheltered area away from the wind and rain.

8. To many, a patio is not a patio without a barbecue. You can either build a barbecue as part of the patio or use a mobile unit.

9. While the adults are relaxing outdoors, it is often desirable to have the children playing nearby. Provide for a game area for the youngsters, teen-agers and adults. The play area for young children should be close enough so that they can be supervised but far enough away so that they are not disturbing.

10. Shrubs and attractive plantings help make outdoor living more attractive and relaxing.

11. With certain patios, a fireplace is needed, particularly on cooler evenings. If you live in such a locality, plan on building a fireplace as part of the outdoor living area.

12. The patio floor should be durable, easy to clean, attractive, easy to walk on, quick-drying, glare-free and non-skid.

13. Some provision for outdoor storage is necessary. Even with a patio built adjoining the house, it's

1724

Photograph courtesy of Alsynite Company of America.

Pebbly-concrete combined with slick concrete produces a striking pavement for this patio. Note that the wood fence for privacy is combined with an overhead wooden frame with plastic fiberglass panels to provide necessary shade for the outdoor living area.

handy to have some place outdoors to keep cooking equipment, game supplies and other outdoor items.

Dining on the patio is a special warm-weather delight. Furniture here is of expanded aluminum—lightweight, durable and easy to store in winter.

Patio Pavements

There are many different types of paving materials you can use for your outdoor living center. Each of the materials has its own advantages and shortcomings. Which you select will depend to some extent upon how much you wish to spend on your patio and the effect you wish to achieve.

Who says a concrete patio has to be dull? This couple painted theirs to match the weathered brick of their front walkway.

Concrete is frequently used for it can be poured easily by the home-owner. You can color it, if you wish, and finish it in different ways, from a smooth slick surface to a pebbly surface. However, it must be laid properly or you may have difficulty later. See *CONCRETE*.

Flagstones are probably the most expensive of all patio paving materials. However, they cannot be matched for their performance or beauty. They are very rugged but some people find it difficult to lay them in pleasing patterns and color arrangements. See section *PATIO—FLAGSTONE*. Frequently slate is used in place of flagstone; it is quite durable but considerably less expensive.

Bricks are also very popular and provide a pleasing, skid-proof surface. They are simple to lay and can be set either in a bed of sand or concrete, but when laid in sand, there is the possibility of their heaving during cold weather. Furthermore, they stain easily and may split under excessive weight or a sharp blow. In addition, you cannot use brick as a surface if you want an outdoor dancing area. See section *PATIO—BRICK*.

Concrete Blocks are available in many colors and are usually made 8″x16″ and 2″ thick. Of course, you can make your own blocks with regular or ready-mix concrete. These blocks can be laid in the same manner as brick in sand. They are as durable as concrete but, unless set on a properly laid base, they are likely to heave during cold weather.

Tiles come in a variety of colors, shapes and sizes and can be made into a very attractive patio. They are particularly effective in homes where the outdoor living area is an extension of indoor living space, separated by sliding glass doors. The tiles must be laid in concrete and you must be extra careful to avoid staining them with mortar as you set them in place. See *TILES*.

Asphalt is the least expensive of all the patio paving materials. If laid properly, it can be durable. The homeowner can lay asphalt in small quantities at a time as the material comes already mixed and can be purchased at some hardware stores, building supply yards and even lumber yards. However, asphalt is affected by heat and under the hot sun it becomes soft and tacky. It is not recommended for hot patios in any section of the country.

Other Materials that can be used for patios include gravel, tanbark, crushed brick, adobe block and even compacted sand. Look all the materials over and then make your choice of the material best suited for your needs.

There's nothing quite as handsome as a formal garden setting with the warm earthy color of brick to complement it. The planter boxes are an ingenious way to blend the stairs into the landscape.

Photo courtesy Structural Clay Products Institute

This handsome pair of concrete patios blend the indoor scene with the outdoors by virtue of the fact that they extend literally through the building wall. Both have common ground in their use of 2x4's as dividers between the concrete areas. The one with the wrought iron furniture in the foreground is finished with exposed fine aggregate. The other is smooth-troweled and edged at each 2x4. Many variations are possible in finishing concrete, depending on the mix used and the degree of finishing with a trowel. *Photos courtesy of Portland Cement Association*

What should you look for when selecting a paving material for your patio? Here are several checkpoints to consider before you select the material:

1. A good paving material should be durable. It should be weather-resistant so that it doesn't melt in the hot sun or buckle or crack in the cold weather.

2. The pavement should be comfortable to walk on. It should not be hot underfoot in the hot summer, nor should it be soft and gummy.

3. The material should harmonize with the material used for your home exterior. Pay particular attention to its texture.

4. The paving material should be easy to clean, preferably by washing off with a garden hose.

Furthermore, it should not require frequent repairs.

6. The surface, although relatively smooth, should be glare-free and skid-proof. Soft-looking materials are usually more attractive than the hard and slick surfaces.

7. Remember price when you are selecting material. The patio usually has to be of reasonable cost. You will find that asphalt is about the cheapest while colored, matched-cut flagstones are the most expensive.

8. When building your own patio, consider the problem of material handling when selecting a paving surface. Some types of patio pavements are easy to install by yourself; others require special equipment and helping hands.

1728